Clear Light of Bliss
Mahamudra in
Vajrayana Buddhism

Geshe Kelsang Gyatso

Translated by Tenzin Norbu
Edited by Jonathan Landaw
with Chris Kolb

Wisdom Publications · London

First published in 1982.

Wisdom Publications
291 Brompton Road,
London SW3, England.

ISBN 0 86171 005 3

Cover painting and illustrations
by Andy Weber.

Typeset in Plantin 11 on 13 point
by Setrite and printed and bound
by Cameron Printing Co. Ltd.,
Hong Kong.

Contents

List of Illustrations

Cover Vajradhara (Tib. Dorje-chang). As holder of the diamond sceptre (vajra), Vajradhara symbolizes the attainment of enlightenment through the union of simultaneous great bliss and emptiness.

Page 2 Vajradhara and consort.

Page 68 Manjushri (Tib. Jam-pel-yang). Depicted holding the sword of discriminating wisdom and the *Perfection of Wisdom Sutra*, Manjushri is the embodiment of the enlightened wisdom of all buddhas.

Page 146 Je Tsong-khapa (1357-1419). The great revitalizer of Buddhism in Tibet, Losang Dragpa received these mahamudra teachings directly from Manjushri. Along with Long-chen Rab-jam-pa (1308-1364) and the Sakya Pandita (1182-1251), Tsong-khapa is considered to have been an emanation of Manjushri himself.

Page 184 Je Phabong-khapa (1878-1941), Trinley Gyatso, was the root guru of both the Senior and Junior Tutors to His Holiness the Fourteenth Dalai Lama and holder of many sutra and secret mantra lineages.

Page 228 Yong-dzin Trijang Dorje-chang (1901-1981), Losang Yeshe, was the Junior Tutor to His Holiness the Fourteenth Dalai Lama and holder of this mahamudra lineage, the *Six Practices* of Naropa, the Lam-rim stages of the path and many other lineages of sutra and secret mantra.

Page 235 Yong-dzin Ling Dorje-chang (1903-   ), Thubten Lungtog is the Senior Tutor to His Holiness the Fourteenth Dalai Lama and holder of this mahamudra lineage. He is the current holder of the throne of Ganden.

Dedication

Through the force of composing this text I send forth the prayer that all fighting among the nations of this planet may immediately come to an end. May the dangers afflicting humankind be pacified quickly. May every embodied being without exception remain forever in peace. May the pure teachings of sutra and secret mantra flourish throughout the world so that all may reach the ultimate peace and happiness of full enlightenment.

And may the reincarnation of the most holy guru, Yong-dzin Tri-jang Dorje-chang, appear quickly for the sake of buddha-dharma and sentient beings.

YONGZIN LINGTSANG

Foreword

OM Bliss and Excellence!

Respectfully and with a devoted mind I follow Losang Dragpa:[1]
the one precious eye of countless migrating beings,
the manifestation of the wisdom of countless omniscient buddhas
and possessor of three beautiful sets of vows.

This magnificent commentary on the Joyous mahamudra[2]—
Derived from churning the essence of the tantric text ocean
That developed from the heart of the most precious guru—
Is published with the pure wish to benefit migrators.

By its publication may all three worlds be beautified
By the numberless benefits of happiness coming from the
   impeccable
And splendid teachings and practices of Losang Dragpa,
Whose treasure-like tradition of the Conqueror resembles a
   wish-granting gem.

May all the beings and communities following buddhadharma
Remain for a long time with their enlightening deeds increasing.
May all sangha members uphold pure discipline as their acts
   of benefit grow full.
May all disease, wars, famine and afflictions be pacified
And may everyone in this world enjoy happiness, joy and glory.

May all beings, equal in number to the vastness of space,
Never be separated from precious teachers throughout their
   lives.
Like the waxing moon, may everything excellent increase in
   accordance with dharma
Any may everyone speedily achieve the ultimate enlightenment
   of Vajradhara.

I am very happy to learn that Venerable Geshe Kelsang Gyatso has given lengthy secret mantra teachings based on the Protector Manjushri Je Tsong-khapa's great treatises and other authentic commentaries on mahamudra, including the root text of the First Panchen Lama.

May these teachings, originally given at Manjushri Institute in England and now made available in this text, *Clear Light of Bliss*, be a source of great happiness and immeasurable benefit to all the human beings of this world.

May all virtue and excellent qualities increase!

Yong-dzin Ling Rinpoche
Ninety-seventh Holder of the
Throne of Ganden
Tutor to His Holiness the
Fourteenth Dalai Lama

Preface

There were many reasons motivating the effort put into composing this text on secret mantra mahamudra. I intended this work to be of direct benefit to western students of Buddhism and I hoped that indirectly it would prove beneficial to all beings.

As for the manner of its composition, this text is based upon my slight experience gained through the kindness of my holy gurus from whom I received instructions on the generation and completion stages of secret mantra practice. In addition, it is based on the teachings found in many standard texts and commentaries. These include Je Tsong-khapa's *Lamp Thoroughly Illuminating the Five Stages*—the essence of this great lama's secret mantra teachings—and his commentary to the *Six Practices* of Naropa. I have also consulted the First Panchen Lama's root text on mahamudra, *Main Path of the Conquerors,* and his autocommentary, *Lamp of Re-illumination,* as well as the mahamudra texts of Kachen Yeshe Gyaltsen and Keu-tsang and many other authentic works on secret mantra. Because I have incorporated the teachings of such profound masters, there is some reason to hope that this present contribution will be of significant benefit to its readers.

However, to achieve the pure realizations of mahamudra it

is not enough merely to read these instructions. First you must train in the stages of the path common to both sutra and secret mantra as presented in such works as Gampopa's *Jewel Ornament of Liberation* and Tsong-khapa's *Great Exposition of the Stages of the Path*. It is also important to perform the four mahamudra preliminary practices (Tib. ngön-dro) in order to clear away obstacles and accumulate meritorious energy. Once you have received some experience of renunciation, the enlightened attitude of bodhicitta, the correct view of emptiness and so forth, you are qualified to receive the empowerments of highest yoga tantra after which you must be careful to keep the appropriate mantric pledges purely. Finally, having attempted to receive the experience of the generation stage practices you should ask for instructions on mahamudra from a qualified spiritual master. If you perform all these prerequisites meticulously and then practise these secret mantra teachings with both faith and wisdom, it is definite that you will attain the realization of mahamudra union.

The importance of engaging in these preliminary trainings and having an impeccable motivation before attempting to practise secret mantra mahamudra has been emphasized by the masters of all Tibetan traditions of Buddhism. Using the instructions contained in this present text for purposes of business or personal gain or having any other similarly debased motive will, far from conferring the desired profit or power, merely expose one to many dangers. As Buddha Vajradhara stated in many tantric treatises, the unfortunate results of misusing these teachings include physical illness, a shortened lifespan, mental obscurations, descent into states of lower migration and the like. Therefore, it is necessary to keep in mind that such advanced methods of spiritual discipline should not be used selfishly merely to enhance the temporary welfare of this life but should be directed to the attainment of highest enlightenment for the benefit of all.

Acknowledgements

The teachings presented here were originally delivered in

1980 as lectures at Manjushri Institute in Ulverston, England. They were compiled through the kind and persistent efforts of Chris Kolb who produced the initial draft of the manuscript upon which this present volume is based. This draft version was then translated back into Tibetan by Tenzin Norbu, at which time the author extensively revised his original presentation with the view of making it more accessible to the reading public. This revised manuscript was edited for final publication by Jonathan Landaw. This final version was rechecked and revised with the assistance of Sharon Gross.

At various stages the task of typing the manuscript was undertaken by Truus Philipsen, Aleca Moraites and Wendy Chatfield in addition to the above-mentioned compilers. The final draft was completely retyped by Susan Horne and the entire presentation was designed by Robina Courtin. To all of these dedicated students and to everyone else involved in taping, translation, editing, design and production the author wishes to convey his heartfelt appreciation and thanks.

Clear Light of Bliss

Mahamudra in
Vajrayana Buddhism

Vajradhara and consort

Introduction and Preliminaries

It is very pleasing to have this opportunity to explain the method of practising secret mantra mahamudra according to the mahayana tradition. This explanation will be given under three main headings:

1 The reason why it is necessary to practise secret mantra and the introduction to the general spiritual path
2 An explanation of the authenticity of this mahamudra lineage
3 The actual instructions of this mahamudra

The reason why it is necessary to practise secret mantra and the introduction to the general spiritual path (1)

In his text entitled *A Guide to the Bodhisattva's Way of Life*, Shantideva states:

By depending upon this boat-like human body
You can cross the great ocean of suffering.
In the future such a vessel will be hard to find;
This is no time to sleep, you fool!

Cyclic existence is like a vast ocean and repeated rebirth in it gives rise to suffering just as the ocean gives rise to waves. At this moment you have found a precious human body: the best vessel for crossing this perilous ocean. If you were to waste this precious form and let it be lost without taking full advantage of it, this would be extremely foolish for it will be very difficult to find a similarly endowed form in the future. You would be like the adventurer who waited a long time to find a boat that could carry him to a treasure island. When he finally found such a boat he went to sleep instead of taking immediate advantage of it. How foolish he felt when he woke up to discover that the long awaited vessel had been washed away and he was stranded as before!

Similarly, at this time you have found the boat-like human body that can transport you to the island of buddhahood: complete awakening. If, instead of taking advantage of this body, you were to waste it on the meaningless activities of this life, this would be most tragic. Therefore, you must try to extract the greatest meaning from your present situation. The highest of all possible human goals is the attainment of complete awakening in which all obstacles obscuring the mind have been removed and all beneficial states of consciousness—wisdom, compassion and skilful means—have been fully developed. Such awakening—known as perfect buddhahood or enlightenment—is a state of ultimate peace. However, you cannot reach this ultimate peace merely by waiting for it; you need to use the appropriate methods to take you there.

These methods are the paths of sutra and secret mantra. Other than these two there is no third method for reaching full enlightenment and, of these two, the techniques revealed in secret mantra are superior. Furthermore, secret mantra is not only the supreme path to full awakening, it is also extremely rare. As Je Tsong-khapa has said, the teachings of secret mantra are even rarer than the buddhas. Although a thousand founding buddhas will appear during this world age, it is said that among them only the fourth (Shakyamuni), the eleventh and the last will teach the paths of secret mantra.

At the moment we all have a great opportunity to practise these rare and extremely beneficial teachings so it is important to develop the strong intention to follow them purely. If these mahayana teachings vanish from the world it will be impossible to become a buddha. Therefore, before these teachings disappear you should exert a great deal of effort and try to incorporate these precious methods into your life.

The etymology of secret mantra is as follows. 'Secret' indicates that these practices should be done in private. If you make a display of your practices you will attract many interfering hindrances and negative forces. This would be like a woman who mentions openly and carelessly that she has a precious jewel in her purse. As a result of her thoughtlessness she will attract many people who will try to steal her treasure. As for 'mantra', this means protection for the mind. The function of secret mantra is to carry one swiftly through the stages of the spiritual path by protecting the mind against ordinary appearances and conceptualization.

The body of secret mantra practices and scriptures often goes by the name vajrayana, 'yana' meaning vehicle and 'vajra' meaning indestructible diamond. Here 'vajra' refers to the indivisibility of wisdom and method. Wisdom is the unmistaken understanding of emptiness (shunyata) while, in these teachings, method refers to simultaneous great bliss. Wisdom is the cause of the truth body (dharmakaya) and method the cause of the form body (rupakaya) of a buddha. The union of wisdom and method, being the union of simultaneous great bliss and emptiness, is peculiar to secret mantra and is the quickest way to gain the truth and form bodies of a fully awakened being. To summarize, the vehicle of the indivisibility of wisdom and method is called vajrayana.

Je Tsong-khapa discussed the distinguishing qualities of secret mantra in terms of four attributes known as the four complete purities. These are the complete purities of the environment, one's body, enjoyments and deeds. The practice of these four is found only in secret mantra and not in the sutra teachings. Secret mantra is differentiated from sutra because it employs the yoga (or method of training the mind) that can bring the future result into the present path. For

example, even though you have not yet reached enlightenment, when practising secret mantra you can prevent the
ordinary appearances and conceptualization of the environment from arising and instead visualize your surroundings as
the mandala abode of a buddha. In the same way you can
prevent the ordinary appearances of your body, enjoyments
and deeds from arising and, in their place, generate yourself as
a deity, visualize the enjoyments of a buddha and enact a
buddha's enlightened deeds. By doing such practices you can
reach the resultant state of buddhahood very rapidly. In both
the generation and completion stages of secret mantra these
four practices are very important and form the foundation for
the teachings presented in this book, such as the meditations
on inner fire (Tib. tum-mo). Furthermore, whenever you do
any secret mantra meditation you must generate the fully
qualified—or at least the superficial—bodhicitta motivation,
wishing to attain buddhahood for the sake of others.

Secret mantra is divided into four sets of tantra: action
(kriya), performance (charya), union (yoga) and highest union
or highest yoga (maha-anuttara-yoga) tantra. As indicated by
their titles, in the first class of tantra emphasis is placed
mainly upon one's external actions, in the second emphasis is
placed equally upon external actions and internal yoga, in the
third internal yoga is mainly stressed, while the highest yoga
tantra is the supreme of all systems of yoga.

All four levels of secret mantra utilize the transformation of
great bliss into the spiritual path but the methods of transformation differ according to the level being practised. The
action tantra meditator tries to generate great bliss by looking
at a visualized goddess and it is this great bliss that is transformed into the path. In performance tantra, in addition to
looking at an appealing goddess, the meditator visualizes that
she is smiling. As before the great bliss generated in this
fashion is brought into the path. In union tantra, in addition
to exchanging glances and smiles with the goddess, the meditator tries to develop great bliss by visualizing holding hands
with her and so forth. Finally, in highest yoga tantra the med-

itator tries to generate great bliss either by sexually embracing an actual consort or by visualizing such an embrace and it is this bliss that is then transformed into the path. It should be understood, however, that it is very difficult to use great bliss as a way of reaching enlightenment. If you are able to do so you have indeed achieved a formidable accomplishment. As was stated by the great mahasiddha Saraha, 'Everyone is excited by copulation but very few can transform that bliss into the spiritual path.'

It is generally taught in Buddhism that attachment is a delusion and therefore must be abandoned. In secret mantra, however, there is a method for transforming attachment into the path but to practise that method one must be very skilful. This skill entails having one's attachment become the cause of experiencing great bliss and then using the mind of that great bliss to meditate upon emptiness. Only if one can do this is it a transformation of attachment. Attachment itself, because it is a delusion, cannot be used directly as a path. Even in secret mantra it should ultimately be abandoned. The true practice of secret mantra, in which the bliss arising from attachment meditates on emptiness, overcomes *all* the delusions, including attachment itself. It is similar to the fire produced from rubbing two pieces of wood together; that fire eventually consumes the wood from which it arose.

For those who are unskilful or whose minds are untrained, such practices of transformation are impossible. For this reason the yogis[3] and meditators of the past have said that in order to reach the realizations of secret mantra one's mind should first be controlled by training and practising in the sutra stages of the path. Without building this firm foundation there is absolutely no way to reach the flawless understanding of secret mantra.

Revealing these teachings of secret mantra can be dangerous for both the spiritual master and the disciple if they are not properly qualified. At the very least they should have the appropriate motivation. A teacher should reveal these methods only out of the great compassionate intention to have the holy dharma flourish for the benefit of others. Should someone reveal these meditations motivated by attachment to the happiness of this life—wishing to achieve fame, gifts and so forth—this would be the cause for that person to take rebirth in the deepest hell.

It is also dangerous for the disciple to receive the empowerments and hidden instructions of secret mantra if he or she practises without keeping the appropriate pledges, wishes only an increase in reputation, possessions and so forth or merely desires to collect information for an academic course. Any of these or similar worldly motivations will lead to nothing but future suffering for such a misguided person.

It is very important that both spiritual master and disciple should have controlled minds and impeccable motivation. Even though you may call yourself a buddhist and take refuge in the triple gem of buddha, dharma and sangha everyday, these are insufficient qualifications for the practice of secret mantra. It is also imperative that you generate the highest of all motivations—the precious mind of bodhicitta—and dedicate yourself and your practices to attaining full enlightenment solely for the purpose of benefiting others. Therefore, whenever you meditate on secret mantra, you should begin by reciting from the heart the following four-lined prayer:

> I shall drink the nectar of this teaching
> To attain buddhahood within this life
> Through the profound path of secret mantra
> For the sake of every sentient being.

Now follows an introduction to mahamudra in general and to the organization of this text in particular. Mahamudra is a Sanskrit term composed of two parts, 'maha' meaning great and 'mudra' meaning seal. In the sutra mahamudra system, great seal refers to emptiness. As Shakyamuni Buddha stated in the *King of Concentrations Sutra*, 'The nature of all phenomena is the great seal.' Here, 'nature' refers to the *ultimate* nature of all things: their emptiness, or lack, of inherent existence. Such emptiness is called the great seal because phenomena never move or change from the state of lacking inherent existence. Since emptiness is the nature of all phenomena it is called 'seal' and since direct meditative realization of it leads to the achievement of the great purpose—complete liberation from the sufferings of cyclic existence—it is also called 'great'.

If someone is a buddhist, he or she should assert the four following irrefutable views, or seals:

(1) all products are impermanent
(2) all contaminated things are miserable
(3) all phenomena are selfless
(4) only nirvana is peace.

Of these four, it is the third which is known as the 'great' seal because it is by realizing that all phenomena are selfless (or empty) that one attains the great purpose of liberation (nirvana).

In the present text, mahamudra meditation is explained not according to the sutra system but in terms of the completion stage of highest yoga tantra. In this system 'great' refers to simultaneous great bliss while 'seal' refers to emptiness itself. Therefore, the actual secret mantra mahamudra is the union of simultaneous great bliss and emptiness.

According to secret mantra, mahamudra is divided into two stages: causal-time and resultant-time mahamudra. The former is the mahamudra practised prior to the moment when actual buddhahood is attained. Thus the time spent on the path leading to full spiritual awakening is causal-time. The resultant-time mahamudra is the union of no more learning and refers to the fruit of buddhahood itself.

Causal-time mahamudra is itself divided into two successive stages: the mahamudra that is the union of simultaneous great bliss and emptiness and the mahamudra that is the union of the two truths. The first union occurs when the subjective simultaneous great bliss realizes emptiness as its object. Objective emptiness is the same in both sutra and secret mantra; what differs is the mind realizing this emptiness. It is in terms of this subjective mind that secret mantra meditation is superior to that of sutra. Realizing emptiness by means of the mind of simultaneous great bliss is the quickest method of attaining full enlightenment.

It should be noted that the simultaneous great bliss of the completion stage of secret mantra is not the ordinary pleasure people experience at the height of sexual embrace. Simultaneous great bliss is experienced *only* when the white drop[4] melts as the result of the practitioner's causing his or her winds to enter, abide and dissolve within the central channel through the force of meditation. Using such simultaneous great bliss to realize emptiness was the essential heart practice of the great secret mantra masters of ancient India such as Saraha, Nagarjuna, Tilopa, Naropa, Maitripa and so forth. It was also the heart meditation of such great Tibetan masters as Marpa, Milarepa, Gampopa, Je Tsong-khapa and so forth. As it was true in the past, it is still true today: the secret mantra meditator's most expedient path to perfect enlightenment is through the union of simultaneous great bliss and emptiness.

The second stage of causal-time mahamudra is the mahamudra that is the union of the two truths: the deceptive and the ultimate. In this text, the pure illusory body is known as the deceptive truth and the meaning clear light is known as the ultimate truth. Assembling these two truths within one person's continuum simultaneously is known as the mahamudra that is the union of the two truths. This mahamudra is the ripened fruit of the mahamudra that is the union of bliss and emptiness. Causal-time mahamudra therefore contains both a cause and a result. Through the force of accomplishing the two-stage causal-time mahamudra you will attain the resultant-time mahamudra, or actual buddhahood, which has the seven features of the father and mother facing one another. This concludes the explanation of the general spiritual path of secret mantra.

An explanation of the authenticity of this mahamudra lineage (2)

Chart 1 *The close mahamudra lineage*

Buddha Vajradhara

Manjushri

Je Tsong-khapa (1357-1419)

Togden Jampel Gyatso (1356-1428)

Baso Chökyi Gyaltsen (1402-1473)

Drubchen Dharma Vajra

Gyalwa Ensapa (1505-1566)

Kedrub Sangye Yeshe (1525-1591)

Panchen Losang Chögyen (1570-1662)

Drubchen Gedun Gyaltsen	Drungpa Tsöndru Gyaltsen
Drungpa Tsöndru Gyaltsen	Losang Dönyö Drubpa
Könchog Gyaltsen	
Panchen Losang Yeshe	Drub-kangpa Geleg Gyatso
Losang Trinley	Phurchog Ngawang Jampa
Drubwang Losang Namgyal	Kun-kyen Jigmey Wangpo
Kachen Yeshe Gyaltsen	
Phurchog Ngawang Jampa	Gung-tang Tenpey Drönmey
Panchen Palden Yeshe	Je-tzun Könchog Gyaltsen
Kedrub Ngawang Dorje	Drubchen Ngödrub Rabten
Ngul-chu Dharmabhadra	
Yangchen Drubpay Dorje	Yong-dzin Gedun Gyatso
Kedrub Tenzin Tsöndru	Palden Tenpey Nyima

Dorje-chang Phabong-khapa Dechen Nyingpo

Yong-dzin Dorje-chang Losang Yeshe Tenzin Gyatso
(Trijang Rinpoche)

Yong-dzin Dorje-chang Thubten Lungtog Namgyal Trinley
(Ling Rinpoche)

All the meditations included within this present text are traceable to Buddha Vajradhara and to the great secret mantra masters of ancient India. These techniques were passed from the Indian to the Tibetan masters and have been handed down to the present day in an unbroken lineage from spiritual father to spiritual son.

Although these meditations were practised in ancient India, this particular system of mahamudra is called a 'close' lineage. This indicates that Buddha Vajradhara transmitted these teachings to Manjushri, the embodiment of enlightened wisdom, who in turn revealed them directly to Je Tsong-khapa. Thus Je Tsong-khapa was the first human master in this particular lineage. (See Chart 1.)

The two branches of this lineage were recombined in Trinley Gyatso, more widely known as Phabongkha Rinpoche, who is considered to have been an emanation of the tantric deity Heruka. This great lama was like the sun of the dharma, illuminating the hidden meaning of both sutra and secret mantra. He passed this mahamudra lineage to his heart son, Yong-dzin Trijang Dorje-chang, the Junior Tutor of His Holiness the Fourteenth Dalai Lama. It is through his kindness and authority that this present text appears.

A prayer to the gurus of this mahamudra lineage is presented as Appendix 1. If you are sincerely interested in studying and practising the meditations presented in this volume, you should receive the blessings of this lineage by reciting that prayer and offering a mandala.[5] Because successful practice depends to a large extent on the blessings and inspiration of the spiritual masters and guides, the wise student will not neglect to recite such prayers.

The actual instructions of this mahamudra (3)

These instructions are given under three headings:

    4 The preliminary practices
    7 The actual practice of mahamudra
  92 The concluding stages

The preliminary practices (4)

In order to perform the practices of mahamudra success-fully, there are two sets of preliminaries to be accomplished:

  5 The four common preliminaries
  6 The uncommon preliminaries

The four common preliminaries (5)

These practices are designed to prepare one for the more advanced techniques of secret mantra. They help cleanse the practitioner of the various obstacles and defilements of body, speech and mind thereby eliminating hindrances that would interfere with successful practice. They also serve to generate a store of positive energy, or merit, that will enable realiza-tions of the more advanced practices to ripen in one's mind. This process of cleansing defilements and collecting meri-torious energy is often compared to the way in which a farmer prepares a field for cultivation, first removing the rocks and the weeds and then nurturing the soil with water, fertilizer and the like. Just as such preparations ensure a successful crop, so does the proper practice of the preliminaries help ensure successful secret mantra meditation.

Briefly listed, these four preliminaries are:

(1) Taking refuge and generating the bodhicitta
    motivation: the gateways to becoming a
    buddhist and a mahayana practitioner
(2) Offering the mandala: the gateway to the
    accumulation of merit
(3) Meditating on and reciting the mantra of Vajra-
    sattva: the gateway to the purification of non-
    virtuous actions and
(4) Practising guru-yoga: the gateway to receiving
    inspiring strength.

If an explanation of these four were given here, this text would become too long. Therefore, those seriously interested in prac-tising mahamudra should consult those works in which these practices are explained and perform them conscientiously.[6]

The uncommon preliminaries (6)

As was mentioned earlier, there are two parts of highest yoga tantra meditation: the generation stage and the completion stage. The techniques of secret mantra mahamudra belong to the completion stage while the various yogas of the generation stage constitute the extraordinary preliminaries. Each highest yoga tantra meditational deity has its own generation stage practices which are explained in great detail in Je Tsong-khapa's *Great Exposition of the Stages of the Path of Secret Mantra* and Kedrub Je's *Ocean of Actual Attainment*.

There is more to the generation stage of secret mantra than merely generating yourself as a particular deity. It is only when you generate yourself as such a deity in conjunction with the yogas of taking the three bodies as the path that you are actually engaged in generation stage practices. If you cannot study the above-mentioned texts in which these yogas are extensively explained, you must at least receive brief instructions on the generation stage from a qualified master in order to practise secret mantra mahamudra. All of this, of course, is based on having first received the appropriate highest yoga tantra empowerment.

If, for example, you have received the empowerment of Heruka, you should first practise the generation stage of the *Heruka Tantra* before engaging in mahamudra. If you cannot study Heruka's generation stage extensively then, for the time being at least, you must do the following abbreviated practice. (Although the following instructions are given in terms of Heruka, they are applicable to other meditational deities such as Vajrayogini, Yamantaka, Guhyasamaja and so forth, provided that the appropriate changes are made with respect to the visualization of the deity, the colours and so forth.)

After sitting on your meditation cushion think: *Unceasingly I go for refuge to all the buddhas, to all the dharma and to all the sangha. I must become Buddha Heruka in this life for the benefit of all sentient beings.* This should be recited three times.

Then instantly visualize: *Every environment and all the beings therein melt into blue light and that light dissolves into me.*

Then my own body dissolves into light and melts from the bottom and top simultaneously, becoming smaller and smaller and eventually dissolving into the blue huṁ *at my heart. The* huṁ *itself gradually dissolves from its bottom into the nada at its top. Finally even the nada disappears, dissolving into the clear light of emptiness.*

At this point strongly think that your mind and Heruka's mind are indistinguishably mixed, like water being poured into water. Focussing on this dharmakaya mind cultivate divine pride by thinking: *This dharmakaya is I myself.* This is the short meditation on taking death to the path of the truth body (dharmakaya). Its main purpose is to release you from ordinary appearances, purify ordinary death, cause the ripening of the clear light of the completion stage and plant the seed to reach the actual truth body of a buddha.

Then visualize: *From the state of dharmakaya emptiness my mind instantly transforms into a blue light a forearm in length, standing vertically upon a sun cushion that rests in the centre of an eight-petalled variegated lotus.* And think: *Now I have become the complete enjoyment body* and develop divine pride as such. This is the short meditation on taking the intermediate state (Tib. bar-do) to the path of the enjoyment body (sambhogakaya). The main purpose of this meditation is to purify the ordinary intermediate state, cause the ripening of the illusory body of the completion stage and plant the seed to obtain the actual enjoyment body of a buddha.

Then continue: *Instantly my mind, in the form of blue light, transforms into Heruka, blue in colour, having one face and two arms, holding vajra and bell and embracing the consort Vajravarahi.* And think: *Now I have become the emanation body* and develop divine pride as such. This is the short meditation on taking rebirth to the path of the emanation body (nirmanakaya). Its main purpose is to cause the ripening of the completion stage practices of the mixings of the emanation body and to plant the seed to reach a buddha's actual emanation body. At this point you can meditate on Heruka's body or you can recite his mantra. If you choose the latter, then focus upon the *hum* in your heart and visualize the mantra around it as you recite.

There is no shorter practice of the generation stage than that which has been given above. All the following mahamudra meditations should be based on having done *at least* these abbreviated generation stage practices.

1 Channels, Winds and Drops

The actual practices of mahamudra (7)

As explained in the introduction to the general spiritual path of secret mantra, the practices of mahamudra are divided into three parts:

   8 The mahamudra that is the union of bliss and
       emptiness
  70 The mahamudra that is the union of the two
       truths
  83 The resultant mahamudra union which has the
       seven features of the father and mother facing
       one another

The mahamudra that is the union of bliss and emptiness (8)

This, the first of the causal-time mahamudra practices, is sub-divided into:

   9 An explanation of the method for generating the
       subjective simultaneous bliss
  44 How to realize the objective emptiness

An explanation of the method for generating the subjective simultaneous bliss (9)

There are two methods involved in generating this simultaneous bliss:

10   Generating simultaneous bliss by penetrating the vital points of your own body
41   Generating simultaneous bliss by penetrating the vital points of another's body

Generating simultaneous bliss by penetrating the vital points of your own body (10)

This is the major subject matter of the next several chapters and is explained under four headings:

11   Recognizing the ten doors through which the winds can enter the central channel
12   An explanation of why the winds may be brought within the central channel by penetrating the vital points through the ten doors
13   An explanation of individual purpose
14   An explanation of the specific inner fire meditation

Recognizing the ten doors through which the winds can enter the central channel (11)

You must know the ten doors through which the winds can enter the central channel because it is impossible to generate simultaneous great bliss without channelizing these winds. These ten are the only doors through which the winds can enter.

Normally, except at the time of death and during sleep, the winds will not enter this channel unless one engages in appropriate meditative practices. Therefore, the secret mantra practitioner generates simultaneous great bliss—for use in meditating upon emptiness—by intentionally bringing the winds into the central channel through any of the ten doors by the force of single-pointed concentration.

First it will be useful to describe the central channel. It

begins at the point between the eyebrows and ascends in an arch towards the top of the head. From there it descends in a straight line ending at the tip of the sex organ. All ten doors are located along the central channel as follows:

(1) the upper tip of the central channel: the point between the eyebrows
(2) the lower tip: the tip of the sex organ
(3) the centre of the crown channel-wheel: located in the apex of the cranium
(4) the centre of the throat channel-wheel: located near the back of the throat
(5) the centre of the heart channel-wheel: located between the two breasts
(6) the centre of the navel channel-wheel
(7) the centre of the secret place channel-wheel, which begins four finger-widths below the navel
(8) the centre of the jewel channel-wheel, located in the centre of the sex organ near its tip
(9) the wheel of wind: the centre of the forehead channel-wheel, having six spokes
(10) the wheel of fire: the centre of the channel-wheel located midway between the throat and the heart channel-wheels, having three spokes

The winds may enter the central channel through any of these ten doors in the same way that the inside of a house can be reached through any of the doors leading from the outside.

To penetrate the vital points of your own body you must concentrate on the channels, winds and the white and red drops. According to secret mantra these three constitute what is called the vajra body. The actual vajra is simultaneous great bliss which arises in dependence upon the channels, winds and drops. Therefore, in this case the result is brought into the present moment by imputing the name of the future result upon the presently existing cause; hence the name 'vajra body'.

You must have intimate knowledge of these three elements if you wish to meditate upon the vajra body. Therefore, what follows is an explanation of the stationary channels, the moving winds and the contained drops.

The stationary channels

There are three main channels (Skt. nadi; Tib. tza): central, right and left. These are like the poles of the six principal channel-wheels. The central channel is pale blue and has four attributes: (1) it is very straight, like the trunk of a plantain tree, (2) inside it has an oily red colour like pure blood, (3) it is very clear and transparent like a candle flame and (4) it is very soft and flexible like a lotus petal.

From the tip of the sex organ up to the top of the head the central channel is very straight, but from there it bends down in an arch and terminates between the two eyebrows. This channel is located exactly midway between the left and right halves of the body but is closer to the back than it is to the front. Immediately in front of the spine is the thick 'life channel' and in front of that is the central channel. Although its most common name is the central channel, it is also known as the two abandonments because gathering the winds into this channel causes the negative activity associated with the winds of the right and left channels to be abandoned. It is also known as the mind channel and as Rahu.

Immediately to either side of the central channel, with no intervening space, are the right and left channels. The right one is red in colour and the left is white. From the navel up to the top of the head these three major channels are straight and adjoining one another. As the left channel continues down below the level of the navel it curves slightly to the right, separating slightly from the central channel and rejoining it at the tip of the sex organ. There it functions to hold and release sperm, blood and urine. As the right channel continues down past the level of the navel it curves slightly to the left and terminates at the tip of the anus where it functions to hold and release faeces and so forth.

Other names for the right channel are the sun channel, the speech channel and the channel of the subjective holder. This last title indicates that the winds flowing through this channel cause the generation of conceptions developed in terms of the subjective mind. Other names for the left channel are the moon channel, the body channel and the channel of the held object. This last title indicates that the winds flowing through this channel cause the generation of conceptions developed in terms of the object.

At various places the right and left channels coil around the central one, thereby forming the so-called channel-knots. The four places at which these knots occur are, in ascending order, the navel, the heart, the throat and the crown of the head. At each of these places, except at the heart level, there is one knot formed by a single coil of the right channel and a single coil of the left. As the right and left channels ascend to these places they coil around the central channel by crossing in front and then looping around it. They then continue upward to the level of the next knot. At the heart level the same thing happens, except that there are three such knots formed by three overlapping loops of each of the flanking channels.

The four places where these knots occur are four of the six main channel-wheels (chakra). As it will be important later on to visualize these channel-wheels clearly, a brief introduction to them will be presented here. At each of the six major channel-wheels a different number of spokes, or petals, branch off from the central channel in the same way that the ribs of an umbrella appear to branch off from the central pole of the umbrella. Thus, at the crown channel—known as the wheel of great bliss—there are thirty-two such petals or channel spokes, all of them coloured white. The centre is triangular with the apex facing forwards. (This refers to the shape of the coiled knot, through which the spokes emanate, as seen from the top.) These thirty-two spokes arch downwards like the ribs of an upright umbrella. The description of this and the three other major channel wheels is given in Chart 2.

Chart 2 *The four major channel wheels*

location	name	shape of centre	number of spokes	colour	direction of arching
crown	wheel of great bliss	triangular	thirty-two	white	downwards
throat	wheel of enjoyment	circular	sixteen	red	upwards
heart	wheel of phenomena	circular	eight	white	downwards
navel	wheel of emanation	triangular	sixty-four	red	upwards

The four major channel-wheels contain a total of 120 spokes. As for the two additional channel-wheels, the secret place has thirty-two red-coloured spokes arching downwards and the jewel channel-wheel has eight white spokes arching upwards. It should also be noted that according to some texts the spokes at the crown, navel and secret place can be visualized as variegated in colour.

The heart channel-wheel is of particular importance and is therefore described in more detail as follows. Its eight spokes, or petals, are arranged in the cardinal and intermediate directions (with the east in front) and in each spoke mainly flows the supporting wind of a particular element as indicated in Chart 3.

Chart 3 *The spokes of the heart channel-wheel*

direction	name of spoke	supporting wind
east	the triple circle	of the earth element
south	the desirous	of the water element
west	the householder	of the fire element
north	the fiery	of the wind element
south-east	channel of form	of the element of form
south-west	channel of smell	of the element of smell

direction	name of spoke	supporting wind
north-west	channel of taste	of the element of taste
north-east	channel of touch	of the element of touch

From each of these eight petals, or channel-spokes of the heart, three channels split off. These twenty-four are the channels of the twenty-four places. They are divided into three groups of eight: those called the channels of the mind are blue and through them mainly wind flows; those of the speech are red and contain mostly blood, or the red drops; those of the body are white and contain mostly white drops. Each channel goes to a different place in the body. As these are the places where one visualizes the body mandala of Heruka, they will be presented here in terms of that male deity. Thus, the outer tips of the eight channels of the mind circle go to (1) the hairline of the forehead, (2) the crown of the head, (3) the right ear, (4) the back of the neck, (5) the left ear, (6) the place between the eyebrows, (7) the two eyes and (8) the two shoulders. Those of the speech circle go to (9) the two armpits, (10) the two breasts, (11) the navel, (12) the tip of the nose, (13) the mouth, (14) the throat, (15) the heart—the area midway between the two breasts—and (16) the two testicles. Finally, those of the body circle terminate at (17) the tip of the sex organ, (18) the anus, (19) the two thighs, (20) the two calves, (21) the eight fingers and eight lesser toes, (22) the front of each ankle, (23) the two thumbs and the two large toes and (24) the two knees.

Each of these twenty-four channels splits into three branches differentiated in terms of the elements—wind, red and white drops—mainly flowing through them. Each of these seventy-two then splits into a thousand so that there are 72,000 channels permeating the body. It is important for the secret mantra practitioner to be familiar with the branching and rebranching of these channels since, as will be explained later, it is through gaining control over the winds and drops flowing through these channels that the union of simultaneous great bliss and emptiness is achieved.

At the present time the winds in the body of an ordinary person flow through most of these channels *except* the central one. Because these winds are impure the various minds they support are also impure. Therefore, as long as the winds continue to flow in the peripheral channels they continue to activate the various negative conceptions that trap beings in cyclic existence. Through the force of meditation, however, these winds can be brought into the central channel. There they are no longer able to support the development of the conceptions of dualistic appearance and thus it is possible to gain a direct intuitive realization of ultimate truth, or emptiness. A more detailed explanation of the visualization and the means of controlling the channels, winds and drops will be given later.

The various locations making up the Heruka body mandala are known as the twenty-four inner places. Corresponding to them are the twenty-four outer places located at various points in the world. People with pure karma can see these outer places of Heruka as pure lands; those with impure karma see them as ordinary geographical locations.

The moving winds
Now follows an explanation of the winds (Skt. prana; Tib. lung). In contrast to the stationary channels they are known as the moving winds because they flow through the channels. Some people believe that only blood and so forth flows through the channels of the body but this is not so. It is owing to the movement of the winds—which, it should be remembered, are much subtler than the external air of the atmosphere—that the circulation of the blood, etc. takes place. If there were no movement of these winds, the other systems of circulation could not function.

There are five root and five branch winds. The root winds are:

(1) the life-supporting wind
(2) the downward-voiding wind
(3) the upward-moving wind

Chart 4 *The root winds*

	life-supporting	downward-voiding	upward-moving	equally-abiding	pervading
colour	white	yellow	red	green/yellow	pale blue
buddha family	Akshobhya	Ratnasambhava	Amitabha	Amoghasiddhi	Vairochana
element	water	earth	fire	wind	space
seat	heart	the two lower doors: the anus and the sex organ	throat	navel	both the upper and lower parts of the body, mainly the 360 joints
function	to support and maintain life	to retain and release urine, faeces, semen, blood, etc.	to speak, swallow, etc.	to cause the blazing of the inner fire, digest food and drink, etc.	to enable the body to come and go; to allow movement, lifting and placing
direction	from both nostrils, gently downwards	from both nostrils, horizontally forwards heavily	from the right nostril, violently and upward	from the left nostril, moving to the left and right from the edge of this nostril	this wind does not flow through the nostrils except at the time of death

    (4) the equally-abiding wind
    (5) the pervading wind

and the five branch winds are:

    (6) the moving wind
    (7) the intensely-moving wind
    (8) the perfectly-moving wind
    (9) the strongly-moving wind
  (10) the definitely-moving wind

Each of the five root winds has six characteristics or attributes by which it can be recognized. Thus each wind has (a) its colour, (b) its associated buddha family, (c) an element for which it serves as the support, (d) its principal seat or fundamental location, (e) its function and (f) its direction, referring to how it leaves the nostrils upon exhalation. The six attributes of each wind are summarized in Chart 4.

If you become familiar with these attributes you will be able to recognize which wind is arising. This ability becomes important at a later stage of meditation. As mentioned above, each root wind serves as the support for a particular element. The first is known as the wind of the water element because it is responsible for the increase of blood, sperm and other liquids in the body. In a similar fashion the wind of the earth element is responsible for the growth of the bones, teeth and nails. The third wind is that of the fire element and as such increases the bodily heat. The fourth increases the flow of the wind element through the channels and the fifth, the wind of the space element, causes an increase in the size of the internal spaces and cavities of the body and is thereby related to growth.

As for the five branch winds, these are so entitled because they all branch off from the life-supporting wind residing in the heart centre. They each flow to the door of a particular sense organ, thereby enabling the consciousness of that organ to move or turn to its appropriate object. The colour and function of each branch wind are summarized in Chart 5.

Chart 5 *The branch winds*

name	colour	function
the moving wind	red	to enable the visual consciousness to move to sights
the intensely-moving wind	blue	to enable the auditory consciousness to move to sounds
the perfectly-moving wind	yellow	to enable the olfactory consciousness to move to smells
the strongly-moving wind	white	to enable the gustatory consciousness to move to tastes
the definitely-moving wind	green	to enable the tactile consciousness to move to bodily sensations

Of these ten root and branch winds, the most important for secret mantra meditation is the life-supporting wind. There are three levels of this wind: the gross, the subtle and very subtle. It is the very subtle wind that travels from life to life and mounted upon it is the very subtle mind; they are interdependent and always together. Since these two never separate the very subtle wind is called indestructible. This indestructible wind is situated in the vacuole, or very small vacuum hole, in the central channel of the heart channel-wheel. It is enclosed in the very centre of the small sphere formed by the very subtle white and red drops.

It is essential to have intimate knowledge of the life-supporting wind for it is the object of meditation when performing such completion stage practices as vajra recitation. Vajra recitation meditation is done within the heart channel-wheel and is a method to loosen the knots of the heart. Such loosening is absolutely necessary if your mahamudra practice is to be successful.

The contained drops

There are two types of drops (Skt. bindu; Tib. tig-le) in the body: the white and the red. The former is the pure essence of the white seminal fluid; the latter is the pure essence of the blood. There are both gross and subtle forms of these white and red drops. Those inside the vacuole of the central channel of the heart are the subtle ones, while the gross red and white drops flow through the other channels. When these drops melt and flow through the channels they give rise to the experience of bliss.

The principal seat of the white drop (also known as the white bodhicitta) is the crown of the head and it is from here that the white seminal fluid originates. The principal seat of the red drop is the navel and it is from here that blood originates. The red drop at the navel is also the foundation of the warmth of the body and the basis for attaining the inner fire.

The channels, winds and drops are the bases for attaining simultaneous great bliss for those who are secret mantra meditators. If a being's body is not endowed with these three there is no opportunity to practise highest yoga tantra. That is why the human body is considered such an excellent form; it is the perfect vehicle with which to perform the secret mantra meditations. Anyone who wishes to practise highest yoga tantra must necessarily be a womb-born human being having the six elements: earth, water, fire, wind, channels and drops. Or, according to another way of listing these elements, one must have bone, marrow and seminal fluid obtained from the father and flesh, blood and skin obtained from the mother.

This concludes the present explanation of the first essential knowledge: knowing the ten doors and the system of channels, winds and drops. More information about them will be given later.

An explanation of why the winds may be brought within the

central channel by penetrating the vital points through the ten doors (12)

To bring the winds into the central channel you must perform those technical meditations that focus your concentration at any of the ten doors mentioned above. The practices of Heruka, Guhyasamaja, Vajrayogini and so forth contain different technical methods for penetrating these points. In some, concentration is focussed at the centre of the heart channel-wheel. In others the centre of the navel channel-wheel is the object on which concentration is focussed. In yet others the winds are brought into the central channel by focussing on the upper and lower ends of the central channel. According to the system set forth in the *Six Practices* of Naropa, the winds enter the central channel through the door of the navel channel-wheel. The present system of mahamudra meditation also utilizes the door of the navel channel-wheel. When you gain confidence that the winds can enter the central channel through the navel channel-wheel, you will also know how they can enter through the other nine doors.

As mentioned before there are sixty-four spokes in the emanation-wheel of the navel. The central, right and left channels ascend through the hub of this channel-wheel, the right and left each coiling around once to form the knot there. In the centre of this knot, inside the central channel, there is a small vacuole similar to a small air bubble. This vacuole is the point or the place to penetrate when meditating on the inner fire. While performing inner fire meditation you must focus your concentration on this vacuole and clearly visualize therein the letter *short a*. Concentrating single-pointedly upon this *short a* is known as penetrating the vital point of the navel channel-wheel of the vajra body. If you visualize your mind as indistinguishably mixed with the *short a* and perform this meditation again and again with strong and steady concentration, you will be successful in bringing the winds into the central channel through the navel channel-wheel.

Why will such meditation cause the winds to enter the central channel? The reason is that the winds automatically gather wherever the mind is placed. This is because the mounted winds and the minds that mount them are inseparable in the same way that the body and its shadow are inseparable. Just as the shadow goes wherever the body goes so too do the winds gather wherever the mind is placed. Focussing the mind in the vacuole within the central channel necessarily causes the mounted winds of that mind to enter the central channel through that vacuole as well. Consistently strong and repeated meditation will gradually cause the central channel to open. This explains how the winds may be brought into the central channel through the navel channel-wheel and the same knowledge can be applied to understanding how these winds may enter through any of the other nine doors.

As stated earlier, it is essential to be very accurate when penetrating the vital points. They are located at the exact centre of the hub of the spokes of the channel-wheels inside the central channel. Sometimes, instead of the *short a*, other letters can be visualized within the vacuoles. In some meditations a *raṁ* is visualized at the navel, in others a *huṁ* or a tiny drop is visualized at the heart, and so forth.

When this meditation of penetrating the vital points is done while holding the vase breath, it is a very quick method to gather the winds within the central channel. When this happens, simultaneous great bliss can be generated without difficulty. When the winds are in the central channel they are very beneficial and enhance the experience of realization. Furthermore, at such times your meditative concentration will be very powerful and penetrating. In normal daily life, concentration is scattered because the winds are moving in the right and left channels, giving rise to conceptual thoughts which interfere with single-pointed concentration. When the winds are in the central channel, however, they will not support such conceptual thoughts. All such conceptualizations are pacified and thus all interruptions are removed. Whatever you choose to meditate upon can be held with unmoving concentration.

An explanation of individual purpose (13)

In general it makes no difference which of the ten doors of the vajra body you penetrate. Any wind may be brought into the central channel through any of the ten doors. However, during the completion stage each channel-wheel performs a different function. If you penetrate the vital point of the crown channel-wheel, the white drops will be increased. If the vital points of the other channel-wheels are penetrated, the results will be as follows: penetrating that of the throat makes dream practices very powerful, of the heart enables you to maintain the vision of clear light, of the navel increases the inner fire, of the secret place gives the experience of strong bliss and, lastly, by penetrating the vital point of the channel-wheel that is located at the tip of the sex organ the experience of strong bliss will be enhanced and a quick, deep and long sleep will be induced.

Why is the last-named ability important? Secret mantra meditators wishing to use sleep as a spiritual path should fall asleep quickly and sleep for an extended period of time. Therefore, they sometimes penetrate the vital point of the sex organ channel-wheel just before falling to sleep and during this protracted sleep they practise the completion stage. However, if you cannot practise the completion stage during waking moments, you will be unable to practise it while asleep. And if you are unable to practise during sleep, you will be unable to practise when it is most important: during the death process. This is because in many respects sleep and death are very similar.

It is very important to practise the completion stage at the time of death. Starting then you must be able to take (1) the clear light of death to the path of the truth body, (2) the intermediate state to the path of the enjoyment body and (3) the ensuing rebirth to the path of the emanation body. These are prepared for by completion stage practices done during sleep when (1) the clear light of sleep is taken to the path of the truth body, (2) dreaming is taken to the path of the enjoyment body and (3) awakening is taken to the path of the emanation body. (See sections 33 and 37.) Therefore, the secret mantra meditator strives to remain within and meditate during the experience of the clear light of sleep.

All ordinary people have a very brief experience of the clear light of sleep but they are unable to recognize and maintain this experience. Clear light is potentially within everyone. The object is to develop the mind of clear light and use this experience as the spiritual path.

Finally, it should be mentioned that it is not necessary to penetrate the vital point of the sex organ channel-wheel only before falling asleep. You may penetrate it at any time in order to bring the winds into the central channel.

2 Inner Fire

An explanation of the specific inner fire meditation (14)

According to the present system of mahamudra meditation the winds are brought into the central channel through the vital point of the navel channel-wheel by the force of inner fire yoga. The yoga of inner fire pervades all completion stage practices. It is the trunk from which all such practices stem and is therefore referred to as the foundation of the completion stage. If something is a completion stage practice, it is either a direct or indirect practice of inner fire. Without igniting and causing the inner fire to blaze and thereby melting the two types of drops, it is impossible to generate simultaneous great bliss.

In general, the completion stage has various objects of meditation. These can be either the channels, the winds, the drops, the inner fire or the letters located within the vital points of the various channel-wheels. Whether a particular practice is a direct or an indirect inner fire meditation is determined by the actual object of meditation. As stated before, inner fire refers to the clear red drop or blood cell residing within the navel channel-wheel. It is called inner fire because it is the nature of heat. If the practitioner visualizes this red blood cell as an actual flame and meditates upon it, that practice is known as a direct meditation on tum-mo.

The Tibetan term 'tum-mo' means 'the fierce one' and is generally used to refer to heroines (Skt. virini; Tib. pa-mo). These heroines, who are slightly wrathful in appearance, bestow simultaneous great bliss on their consorts, the heroes. The red blood cell at the navel in the nature of fire is also called tum-mo because its function is similar to that of the fierce heroines. In this text, however, it will be referred to more descriptively as inner fire.

When practising the yoga of inner fire, you should visualize the clear red blood cell in the form of the syllable *short a*. This letter is called the *short a* of inner fire and, in the practice of mahamudra, meditation upon it is recognized as the best method for initially bringing winds into the central channel. In his teachings Milarepa (1052-1135) very frequently referred to this letter as 'my *short a*'. One day his disciple Gampopa told him that when he practised single-pointed concentration he could remain for seven days in one uninterrupted session. Milarepa replied, 'So what? You sit for seven days and do not experience the clear light. If you meditated upon my *short a* of inner fire you could experience the clear light very quickly.'

By means of inner fire you will quickly be able to attain the single-pointed concentrations of both tranquil abiding (Skt. shamatha; Tib. zhi-nä) and superior seeing (Skt. vipashyana; Tib. lhag-tong) and upon the basis of these two you will attain the example and meaning clear light. Thus the fruits of inner fire meditation are manifold. To compare other methods to inner fire is like comparing a donkey to a fine horse. Although a donkey can carry you to your destination, a fine horse is far superior because of its distinguished qualities. The same is true of the yoga of inner fire.

The practice of inner fire was first elucidated by Vajradhara in the *Hevajra Root Tantra*. From there it was grafted on to other practices such as Yamantaka, Guhyasamaja, Chakrasamvara (Heruka) and Vajrayogini. Thus all the tantric meditators look upon the *Hevajra Tantra* as an especially blessed scripture. Because the inner fire practices come directly from

Vajradhara, who explained them extensively in the root and commentarial texts of the *Hevajra Tantra*, it is practised within all Tibetan buddhist traditions. As the First Panchen Lama (1570-1662) stated in his mahamudra auto-commentary, 'If you can bring the winds into the central channel through the force of habits formed in previous lives, this is very good. Otherwise, the yoga of inner fire as expounded in the *Six Practices* of Naropa should be performed.'

This has been a general introduction to the practice of inner fire. What follows is a detailed explanation of the methods used to ignite and cause the inner fire to blaze.

If you have the strong wish to follow the path of inner fire, you should do the technical method for attainment (sadhana) everyday. Contained within these technical methods are prayers requesting from the heart the blessings of the root and lineage lamas. Thus first you should visualize your root master in the form of Vajradhara and then around him you should visualize the spiritual masters of the mahamudra lineage. Surrounding them are the buddhas, bodhisattvas, heroes, dakinis, dharma protectors and so forth as described in the *Offering to the Spiritual Master* and elsewhere. After visualizing this field for the accumulation of merit, you should make a long or short mandala offering. Then recite from the heart the following prayer three times:

> I bow down and seek refuge in my master
> And in the sublimely precious triple gem.
> Through the strength of your blessings please inspire
> Success in my practice of inner fire.
> Through the force of completing inner fire
> May I quickly reach the Great Seal union.
> Please make my channels both pliant and smooth;
> Make supple my winds and drops.
> May your blessings grant me quick accomplishment
> Without any trouble or the slightest discomfort.

The last lines of the prayer are recited to eliminate the causes for physical hindrances which can impede your progress and prevent success in your practice. To perform the meditations of the completion stage you must be healthy and have pliant and smooth channels, supple winds and flexible white and red drops. Otherwise you may develop wind diseases (Tib. lung) or other physical illnesses.

After this you should generate the precious mind of bodhicitta which strives unceasingly for the attainment of perfect buddhahood for the sake of all beings. This you can do by reciting the following prayer three times:

> I wish to become within this short lifetime
> A perfected buddha for the sake of all beings.
> Thus now I shall practise the inner fire yoga
> To attain my goal with the greatest of speed.

Both the wishing and venturing stages of bodhicitta are contained within this prayer, the first two lines referring to the former and the last two to the latter. The precious mind of bodhicitta is absolutely essential if the practice of inner fire is to be a mahayana practice. And if a method of meditation is not a mahayana practice, how could it possibly be a vajrayana one? Furthermore, if your meditation on inner fire lacks both refuge and bodhicitta, it can even become a non-buddhist path. To perform the yoga of inner fire for worldly purposes will be of no use as a path to full spiritual awakening. Because there is a great difference in motivation between worldly practices and actual dharma practices, their paths and fruits must also be very different.

After reciting and meditating upon the meaning of the above prayers, you should visualize that the merit field and the lineage masters all dissolve into your root spiritual master Vajradhara. Then, with your palms pressed together at your heart in a gesture of supplication, request the root master to come to the crown of your head. When he arrives there feel that your crown channel-wheel opens. The master then gradually grows smaller until he is thumb-size, enters and descends through the central channel and finally dissolves into the indestructible wind and mind which dwell in the centre of the heart channel-wheel. When he dissolves into this indestructible point at your heart, you should contemplate very strongly that your subtle body, speech and mind have been blessed and consecrated. (As was mentioned before, the subtle body is the very subtle wind upon which is mounted the very subtle mind. The combination of these two possesses the potential to communicate. It is this potentiality that is your subtle speech.)

These meditations on refuge, bodhicitta and receiving the blessings of your spiritual master should be done at the beginning of each session of inner fire practice. Furthermore, it is important that you generate the clear appearance and divine pride of yourself as being your personal deity. During the generation stage this deity may be visualized as having multiple arms, legs and faces. During the completion stage meditations, however, this deity is always seen as having only one face and two arms. For example, if your personal deity is Heruka, during completion stage practices you, as Heruka, will have one face and two arms and will be embracing Vajravarahi.[7]

During completion stage meditation your posture should be impeccable. You should sit in the seven-point posture of Vairochana[8] and realize that each of these seven points has a specific purpose. For many people the vajra position of the legs, in which the feet are placed upon the opposite thighs, is very difficult to hold comfortably. If this is true for you, you should try to maintain this position for a few moments at the beginning of your meditation session and then switch to a position that is more comfortable. This will allow you to grow accustomed to the posture and will also serve as an auspicious sign for your practice. Although the full vajra posture is superior, it is sufficient to sit in any cross-legged position or even in the posture of Tara, that is with one leg extended. But, however you sit, you must be sure that your back is perfectly straight.

The actual explanation of inner fire has two main divisions:

15 Meditation on the eight rounds of inner fire
26 Based on these eight rounds, the experience of
     the four joys and the practice of the nine
     mixings

Meditation on the eight rounds of inner fire (15)
   These eight rounds of meditation have the following de-
scriptive titles:

16 Dispelling the impure winds and visualizing
     your body as hollow
19 Visualizing the channels
20 Training in the passageways of the channels
21 Visualizing the letters
22 Igniting the flame of inner fire
23 Causing the inner fire to blaze
24 Blazing and dripping
25 Extraordinary blazing and dripping

   If you wish to attain the realization of inner fire you should
do so on the basis of these eight rounds. Through the attainment of inner fire you will be able to experience the four joys
and practise the nine mixings. By training in inner fire, the
joys and the mixings you can travel the entire path of
mahamudra meditation and fully accomplish all completion
stage practices. You should not be satisfied with merely
attaining the direct methods of inner fire meditation. In
addition to and upon the basis of this, you should go on to
complete the practices of the four joys and the nine mixings.
Je Tsong-khapa was very clear on this point.

Dispelling the impure winds and visualizing your body
as hollow (16)
   As indicated by its title, the first round of meditation has
two divisions:

17 Dispelling the impure winds
18 Visualizing your body as hollow

These two practices are done to free you from mental and physical hindrances and make your mind and body clear and lucid.

Dispelling the impure winds (17)

This is accomplished by the nine-exhalation purification practice. Begin this practice by pressing the tip of your left thumb against the inside of the root of your left ring finger and then make a fist by closing the four fingers over the thumb. This fist is then placed on the right side of the rib cage so that the arm is draped comfortably across the stomach. The arm is rotated upwards slightly enabling the back of the fist to rest on the body at the level of the right elbow and below the armpit.

With the right hand make a similar fist but extend the index finger. With the back of your extended index finger press the left nostril to block it and gently inhale a full deep breath through your right nostril. While smoothly inhaling visualize the inspiring strength of all buddhas and bodhisattvas entering into you through your right nostril in the form of radiant white light which dissolves into the indestructible wind and mind at the centre of the heart channel-wheel. Remain at the height of inhalation for as long as possible.

To exhale, move your extended right index finger to the right nostril, closing this nostril by pressing it with the front of the finger. Exhale all the air in three equal, successive breaths through the left nostril. While exhaling visualize that all impure winds, particularly those of the left side of the body, are dispelled in the form of inky black smoke.

With your finger still pressing on the right nostril, again inhale slowly, smoothly and deeply. Visualize radiant white light streaming into you through your left nostril, bringing the inspiring strength of all buddhas and bodhisattvas and absorbing into the indestructible drop at the heart. Hold this breath until it becomes uncomfortable. Then move the extended index finger back to the left nostril as before and fully exhale all impure winds through the right nostril in three equal breaths. Visualize that all the impure winds, especially those of the right side of the body, are thereby expelled.

Six of the nine rounds have now been completed. Your hands can now be brought to the meditative equipoise position, palms facing upwards with the right hand resting on the left and the tips of the thumbs touching.

After the final exhalation through the right nostril, breathe in smoothly and deeply through both nostrils while visualizing as before. Then exhale through both nostrils three times. When these three exhalations are complete think strongly that all the channels, winds and drops of the body are very supple and comfortable. This nine-round meditation can be repeated as many times as necessary—even for an entire session. It is very important that you do this meditation with as much single-pointed concentration as possible; only in this way will the practice be truly useful.

Visualizing your body as hollow (18)

The purpose of this round of meditation is to eliminate obstacles and problems arising in relation to your channels, winds and drops. If these three are not functioning properly, it is possible to develop various diseases. Furthermore, those who are new to completion stage meditation can cause their bodily elements to become unbalanced by pushing too hard and exerting too much energy. None of these interferences will occur, however, if you make your channels, winds and drops supple by means of these meditative techniques.

As will be discussed in section 22 below, there are two methods for bringing the winds into the central channel through inner fire meditation: the peaceful and the violent or wrathful. The violent method uses physical force to bring the winds strongly and quickly into the central channel. Although such a method can be very effective, it can also be dangerous, causing an imbalance in your winds as well as mental and physical discomfort. Meditating on your body as being hollow will safeguard against this. It is important to prevent completion stage practices from causing an imbalance in your winds because, if this happens, neither doctors nor medicine will be of any help whatsoever.

The peaceful method for bringing the winds into the central channel may take slightly longer but is a much smoother process. When the winds are centralized in this way they enter the channel very gently and smoothly and without the mental and physical side effects that could result from disturbing the channels, winds and drops. Anyone who can practise this peaceful method successfully does not need to meditate on the body as being hollow, because for that meditator there is no danger of wind or channel diseases.

Je Tsong-khapa explained that the peaceful method is superior to the violent one. He pointed out that not only does it prevent the hindrances mentioned above but it is also a more powerful way of experiencing clear light. The peaceful method enhances single-pointed concentration and therefore, when you practise the four joys detailed below, you move naturally and smoothly from one joy to the next. Furthermore, in the root text of the *Hevajra Tantra* as well as in the commentaries to it, it is stated that even if you meditate on the inner fire by holding the vase breath, you should do this practice in a peaceful manner.

Finally, there is one more disadvantage of the violent method that should be mentioned here. If you perform these meditations forcefully with much expectation, you may indeed be able to centralise the winds more quickly. However, the amount of physical movement involved in such a forceful technique can interfere with your clear recognition of the eight signs that occur when the winds dissolve into the central channel. And if you do not recognise the first seven signs, it will be impossible to recognise the eighth sign clearly: the actual clear light. For all these reasons, then, the peaceful method is the preferred practice.

As for meditating on your body being hollow, this is done as follows. First you should see your body in its normal form and condition; i.e. made up of skin, flesh, bone, blood and so forth. Then clearly visualize that all the contents of the body melt into light and gradually disappear into emptiness, leaving only your skin which is now like an empty shell. When this meditation becomes stable visualize that your skin becomes clear and transparent and, like a rainbow, has no resistence to matter. (Here the point of similarity with a rainbow is its intangibility, not its colouring.) If, during any stage of your practice, you experience trouble from wind disease, you should do this meditation until the difficulty subsides, even if it takes several days or weeks. At the end of these meditation sessions you should resume visualizing your body as that of your personal deity.

This has been a rather short explanation of the first round of inner fire meditation. A more detailed explanation would contain bodily exercises known as the six magical wheels. A full explanation of these can be found in Je Tsong-khapa's commentary to the *Six Practices* of Naropa. As stated earlier, when you are following the peaceful method it is not necessary to do these exercises, although you may if you so desire.

Visualizing the channels (19)

The system of channels has already been described. When you practise the meditations of the completion stage, however, the visualization of these channels differs slightly from the description given above. For example, in the second round of inner fire meditation, the central channel is to be seen exactly as described before, including all the four attributes mentioned above, except that here it ends at the secret place instead of at the tip of the sex organ. To visualize the central channel as terminating at this point facilitates secret mantra meditation.

It was stated before that the right and left channels constrict or strangle the central channel by coiling around it and forming knots at the various channel-wheels. Now, however, you should visualize that these knots are loosened, thereby opening the blockages at the channel-wheels. In actuality the central channel is like a shaft of bamboo which has membranes dividing one section from the next. The knots constricting the central channel are like these membranes. When meditating on the completion stage, you should visualize that all these dividing membranes have been removed. Think that if you stood at the top or bottom of the central channel you would be able to look up or down its full length just as if you were looking up or down an empty elevator shaft. The diameter of this channel can vary. Generally, the thinner you visualize it the better. You may start by seeing the central channel the size of an average drinking straw. (A helpful technique is to begin the session by seeing it as very thick, e.g. the size of your arm. Then see it grow thinner and thinner. Finally, when it reaches the size of a drinking straw, let it remain like this and place your concentration on it firmly.) As your concentration improves and becomes more subtle, you can make it narrower and narrower. This progressive diminution of the size of the central channel can be done over a period of several days. If you are serious about meditating upon inner fire, you should concentrate just upon the central channel for many sessions over many days, weeks or even months.

Then turn your attention to the right and left channels and visualize them clearly as well. The right one is red and the left is white. (Note that the inside of all three channels is red. The colours mentioned before only refer to the outside of the channels. In inner fire meditation the outside of the central channel itself is slightly blue.) From the level of the navel straight up to the crown of the head and then arching down to the point between the eyebrows all three channels are together. From the brow, however, the right and left channels continue downwards until they reach the nostrils. At the level of the navel the right and left channels join, or plug into, the central one, forming at that point a trijuncture. Within the central channel, at the very centre of the two-fold knot of the navel channel-wheel, there is a small vacuole as was described earlier. It is very important to know where this vacuole is located because this is where the actual inner fire meditation takes place. If you do not find the right point your entire meditation on the inner fire will be mistaken.

Once your visualization of the three channels has been

stablized, you should concentrate on the spokes, or petals, of the various channel-wheels. First think that you are in the indestructible drop of the heart channel-wheel. As mentioned before, the centre of the heart channel-wheel is constricted by a six-fold knot (three coilings of each flanking channel). The indestructible drop is within the central channel in the very centre of this knot. In the previous descriptions, the spokes of the heart channel-wheel were seen to emanate from the coiling right and left channels. Now, however, visualize them as connecting directly to the central channel itself.

Imagine that you are actually inside the indestructible drop. Think that if you were to turn on a light it would shine down the corridors of the eight spokes of the heart channel-wheel. Look down these spokes carefully, inspecting each one closely until you can conclude, 'Now I have seen the eight petals of the heart channel-wheel clearly.'

Still remaining within the indestructible drop, travel up to the throat channel-wheel. Thinking that you are within the vacuole of the central channel encircled by the two-fold knot, inspect the corridors of each of the sixteen spokes of this channel-wheel. After you have looked through each one carefully think to yourself as before, 'Now I have seen the sixteen petals of the throat channel-wheel clearly.'

Then travel to the crown channel-wheel and do as before. From within the vacuole there, at the centre of the two-fold knot, inspect the corridors of each of the thirty-two spokes until you can think, 'Now I have seen the thirty-two petals of the crown channel-wheel clearly.'

Finally, travel to the navel channel-wheel. From within the vacuole of the two-fold knot here, look down each of the sixty-four spokes until you are satisfied and think, 'Now I have seen the sixty-four petals of the navel channel-wheel clearly.'

In all these visualizations you should see the channel-wheels as they were described earlier except that the spokes join the central channel directly instead of emanating from the right and left channels. Also, depending on how familiar you are with this practice, you can either leave in or omit the visualization of the various knots. A good way to begin this visualization is to leave out all the knots entirely. Then, when you become skilful enough, add in the two-fold knot at the navel. Later, when your skill in meditation has grown sufficiently, you may include the knots at the other three channel-wheels as well.

When visualizing the system of channels, first concentrate on seeing the central channel clearly. Then stabilize the visualization of the right and left channels and see how they join the central channel at the navel. Next meditate upon the spokes of the various channel-wheels by placing your mind successively in each small vacuole of the central channel at each of the four levels. As mentioned before, if you are to bring the wind into the central channel through the method of inner fire meditation, you must use your mind to penetrate the vital point at the centre of the vacuole of the navel channel-wheel. The importance of absolute accuracy in penetrating the vital points cannot be overemphasized. This meditation on inspecting each channel-wheel thoroughly and then finally penetrating the vacuole at the navel should be done for at least several days.

The Long-döl Lama wrote that there is no more powerful meditation than penetrating the central channel with the bodhicitta motivation. This is because by meditating on the central channel you can gain control over the winds and cause them to enter, abide and dissolve within the central channel. It is on the basis of this that you attain the great bliss of the clear light and it is through meditation on clear light that you will complete the two-fold accumulation of merit and wisdom. The advanced meditators who achieved simultaneous great bliss and the emptiness of clear light did not need to exert great effort in performing physical prostrations or other spiritual practices. Merely by meditating on bliss and emptiness they completed the necessary collections for the attainment of full enlightenment, as attested to in tantric texts. These great meditators simply requested the blessings of their root and lineage lamas and then proceeded with the practices described here.

Training in the passageways of the channels (20)

There are two principal reasons for doing this third round
of meditation. First of all, it helps remove the defects in the
channels, winds and drops, making all three of them very clear
and flexible. This prevents you from contracting diseases
associated with the winds and channels. If these three
elements are supple the body as a whole will also be supple.
This is because the stationary channels and moving winds
pervade the entire body. It is very important for a meditator's
body to be comfortable and flexible because this helps the
mind to become clear and lucid and a clear mind makes
meditation powerful and very beneficial. The second reason
for doing this meditation is that it greatly enhances the clarity
of the channel-wheels visualized in the preceding round of
meditation.

To train in this round of meditation first visualize that your
mind is in the form of the indestructible drop located in the
centre of the heart channel-wheel. This pea-sized drop is white
with a slightly reddish tint and shines brilliantly with a five-
coloured light: white, red, blue, green and yellow. (This light
does not extend a great distance from the drop.) With your
mind concentrated single-pointedly on this drop, strongly
contemplate that it is the essence of the inseparability of your
own mind and the mind of your spiritual master. Identify this
sparkling drop in the centre of the heart channel-wheel as
being you yourself. Decide that as the sparkling drop, you
would like to make a tour of the various channel-wheels.

Now slowly ascend through the central channel to the level
of the throat. Come to rest exactly in the centre of the vacuole
in the centre of the throat channel-wheel. Look down each of
the sixteen corridors and then, as if you were turning on a very
powerful electric light, radiate the five colours, so that they
completely illuminate all the spokes of this channel-wheel.
Feel that this brilliant light corrects all the possible defects in
these spokes, such as their being shrivelled, stuck together,
blocked and so forth. All the spokes which have become stiff,
hard and brittle are made soft, smooth and supple. Think that

the elements flowing within the spokes—the winds, white drops and blood—become very clear, powerful and beneficial. Continue with this visualization until the feeling arises that all the defects in the spokes have been rectified. Then reabsorb the light into the sparkling drop. Now think that you have completed your purpose in visiting the throat channel-wheel and make the decision to visit the crown channel-wheel.

Travel slowly up the central channel and come to rest in the exact centre of the vacuole of the crown channel-wheel. Then proceed as before. Take a good look at each of the corridors of this channel-wheel, radiate the powerful five-coloured light down the thirty-two spokes, correct all the defects as before and, when you feel that the job has been done, reabsorb the light and think that you have accomplished your purpose in visiting this channel-wheel.

Now think that you would like to tour the brow channel-wheel. From your place in the crown, look down the central channel to the brow wheel. At the entrance of the central channel, which is exactly midway between the eyebrows, visualize that there is an opening like the third eye of many vajrayana deities. Then slowly descend to this entrance, coming to rest with half of the sparkling drop inside and half outside this opening. Take a good look inside and outside your body, gazing around in every direction. Radiate the five-coloured light and, as it shines inside, see that it corrects all the defects of the channels in the brow. As the light radiates outside, see it purify all impure environments and annihilate the suffering and the gross and subtle causes of suffering of all sentient beings. When you feel that these purposes have been accomplished, move completely inside so that you no longer protrude halfway out of the third eye opening. You should then remain there for a while.

Then make the decision to return to the heart channel-wheel from where you started. Slowly ascend to the crown and pass through the vacuole there. Then descend slowly through the central channel, passing through the vacuole at the throat and finally coming to rest in the centre of the vacuole in the heart channel-wheel. Think that you now have returned to your main abode. Now that you are here inspect the eight spokes of the heart channel-wheel, radiate the five-coloured light throughout their corridors and purify their defects in exactly the same manner as before. When this work has been completed reabsorb the light and think that now you would like to go to the navel channel-wheel.

Slowly descend through the central channel and come to rest in the vacuole there. Look closely at each of the sixty-four spokes of the navel wheel and again radiate the light, correct all the defects in the channels, winds and drops and think that they all have become very supple, pliant, soft and comfortable. After reabsorbing the five-coloured light remain in the vacuole for some time and remember that this is the principal place for your meditation upon the inner fire.

After remaining in the vacuole of the navel for as long as possible, the indestructible drop returns to its place at the heart. Again think that you returned to your main station and determine to purify all the defilements and correct all the defects of the 72,000 channels pervading the entire body. Radiate the five-coloured light through the eight spokes of the heart channel-wheel and then visualize this light as spreading throughout the eight spokes, the twenty-four channels of the twenty-four places, the seventy-two channels derived from these and finally throughout all the 72,000 channels. This five-coloured radiant light repairs all broken, blocked, shrivelled, tangled and stuck-together channels making those that have become stiff, hard and brittle soft, smooth and supple. All the winds and drops are made perfectly clear and pliant in this way. Finally, reabsorb the light into yourself as the indestructible drop.

There are several ways to do this third round of meditation. You must determine for yourself how much time you wish to spend on each of the various stages. It is possible to spend an entire meditation session on exploring just one of the channel-wheels. If you do this, you can begin the next session where the previous one left off. Eventually, however, when you feel you have completed this round of meditation return to the heart channel-wheel. Of the various channel-wheels to be explored, it is most important that you become familiar with and recognize that of the navel. Thus you should spend much of your time in that channel-wheel but be sure that you acquire a thorough knowledge and experience of the other channel-wheels as well.

In summary, training in the passageways of the channels is somewhat like visiting a museum. First you make the decision to go there. Then you enter the ground floor, which in this case corresponds to the heart channel-wheel. From there you go directly to the first floor. After you have thoroughly inspected the exhibitions on the first floor, you go up to the second. Then, after taking a long look at the objects on exhibition there, you return to the ground floor. After examining the exhibits on the ground floor, you descend to the basement and, when you have finished there, you return to the ground floor in order to leave. Having made this extensive tour of the museum, you should be able to remember clearly all the contents of all the exhibits on each floor.

It is very important that the channels appear clearly in your visualization. To practise the yoga of inner fire of the completion stage you must be able to penetrate the vital point of the navel channel-wheel accurately and skilfully. This is like someone who is chopping wood with an axe. If he is skilful and hits the right place, he will split the wood without much difficulty or effort. On the other hand, if he misses the proper place he will not be successful in splitting the wood even after expending much energy.

Another analogy is afforded by a slaughterer of animals. If this person is very skilful and knows how to sever the proper artery, he will be able to kill the animal quickly and painlessly, even if his only instrument is a tiny needle. However, if he lacks skill, the slaughter may turn out to be a long and bloody affair. In a similar fashion, the completion stage meditator who wishes to bring the winds into the central channel will be successful if he or she can penetrate the vital points skilfully.

As a result of such skilful practice, the meditator will acquire supernormal attainments without difficulty.

In order to become familiar with the channels and with the method of penetrating the vital points, and also to correct all the defects of the elements of the vajra body, you should place strong emphasis on training in the passageways of the channels. This you should do for several days or until you have received the experience of clear visualization.

Visualizing the letters (21)

There are extensive and concise explanations of the visualization of these letters. The extensive explanation includes a detailed visualization not only of the letters located in the vacuoles of the navel, heart, throat and crown but also those located at the inner entrances of each of the one hundred and twenty spokes of these four channel-wheels. This extensive explanation will not be given here because it is difficult and not absolutely necessary. You can be completely successful in your practice of inner fire on the basis of the concise explanation alone, which describes only the four letters of the four vacuoles.

First visualize within the vacuole of the crown a round, flat moon cushion made of white light. This cushion is the size of the circular surface formed when a pea is cut in half. Upon this moon cushion is the letter *ham*. It is the size of a mustard seed, white in colour and standing upside down. This letter symbolizes the white drop residing in the crown.

In the vacuole at the throat visualize another moon cushion upon which is the letter *om*.[9] This is also the size of a mustard seed, but is red in colour and stands upright. This *om* symbolizes the red drop at the throat channel-wheel and is in the nature of fire.

In the vacuole of the heart is another moon cushion upon which is the letter *hum*. It is standing upside down, blue and symbolizes the indestructible drop. This is the most subtle drop and does not melt before the time of death.

Finally, in the vacuole of the navel clearly visualize another moon cushion. Upon it, again the size of a mustard seed, is the red letter *short a*. It is standing upright and symbolizes the clear red blood cell residing in the navel. As this is the principal object of concentration when meditating on the yoga of inner fire, and as all the body's warmth is generated from this blood cell, the *short a* should be visualized in the nature of fiery heat.

There are two specific purposes for visualizing these letters in the vacuoles of the central channel at the centre of each channel-wheel. The first purpose concerns the four joys, which will be explained in more detail below. You will be able to experience the four joys when the winds enter, abide and dissolve within your central channel. The longer and more intensely you can hold the experience of each of the four joys, the better your meditation will be. This can be accomplished by visualizing the four letters.

As a result of the meditation described below, the white drop in the crown is made to melt. When it does so it begins to flow down the central channel, eventually passing through the throat, heart and navel channel-wheels and finally reaching the tip of the sex organ. Once the white drop melts, it flows down uninterruptedly. If it flows past a particular channel-wheel without being checked or held there, the experience of joy associated with that channel-wheel will be fleeting and unstable. It is by focussing your concentration on the various letters that you can arrest the downward flow of the white drop and thereby gain a longer and more intense experience of each of the four joys.

The first joy is simply called 'joy' and the experience of it originates in the crown channel-wheel when the white drop residing there melts. Therefore, initially you must meditate for a substantial period of time upon the letter *haṁ* in the crown. The experience of this joy is complete when the white drop reaches the throat channel-wheel by descending through the central channel.

The second joy is called 'supreme joy' and originates in the throat channel-wheel. It is experienced in full when the white

drop reaches the heart channel-wheel. The third joy is called
the 'extraordinary joy' and is experienced in full when the
white drop flowing down the central channel reaches the navel
channel-wheel. Finally, the fourth joy is called 'simultaneous
joy'. It originates in the navel channel-wheel and is experienced in full when the white bodhicitta flows down from
there to the tip of the sex organ. In order to have a sustained
and stable experience of each of these joys, you must have
gained strong control over the downward flowing white drop
and be able to arrest it at each level of its descent. As
explained, this is done by taking the four letters as the objects
of meditation. This concludes the first of the two reasons for
visualizing the letters in the channel-wheels. The second
reason, which will now be explained, is to help you to find the
actual object of meditation in the yoga of inner fire.

The letter *haṁ* is visualized within the vacuole of the crown
channel-wheel. Although its outer appearance is that of a
written letter, you should recognize it as actually being the
white drop in the crown. When you practise the fourth round
of inner fire in meditational retreat, you should begin by
visualizing this white *haṁ* in the crown. Visualize it clearly for
a short while and then move your attention to the red *oṁ* in
the throat. After a while move to the *huṁ* in the heart and
finally settle the mind on the *short a* in the navel channel-
wheel. Visualize the *short a* very clearly and feel it as being in
the nature of powerful, fiery heat. Your concentration should
be focussed on this letter for a longer time than on the others.

Then, after concentrating on the *short a*, move your mind
back to the *huṁ* at the heart, then on to the red *oṁ* in the
throat and finally to the white *haṁ* in the crown. Then move
down again, back to the throat, heart and finally stop at the
navel. Thus you have moved your mind from the crown
downwards, from the navel upwards and then finally from the
crown downwards once again.

At this point your concentration is focussed on the *short a* of
inner fire in the centre of the navel channel-wheel. Visualize
the sixty-four spokes of this wheel and the coiling right and

left channels which form a two-fold knot at the hub of these spokes. In the centre of this knot and inside the central channel is the vacuole of the navel. It is within this vacuole that the tiny moon cushion resides with the letter *short a* standing upon it. This letter is completely pure, infinitely radiant and in the nature of intense fiery heat, red in colour. This is the object of tum-mo meditation. If it is not perceived clearly, your meditation will not be successful. Therefore, this is the time to recall as vividly as possible any other pointing-out instructions that may have been imparted to you by your root spiritual master concerning the location, size, shape, nature and so forth of the *short a*.

Finding the object of meditation depends on recollection and alertness. After finding the object in the manner described above, you should completely dissolve your mind into it. You should concentrate on this object single-pointedly without forgetting it. Once you have accomplished this you have reached the first stage of tranquil abiding meditation, if you have not already reached this state through previous practice. If you meditate continuously, you can gradually reach all nine stages of settling the mind. Thus the *short a* is a unique object of meditation. A single meditation upon it yields four important fruits: achievement of tranquil abiding, channelization of the winds into the central channel, igniting and blazing of inner fire and realization of mahamudra.

The present inner fire meditation is done primarily to bring the winds into the central channel and success in this depends upon perfect concentration. Therefore, whenever you meditate upon the inner fire, you should not see your mind and the object of meditation as being different or dual. As stated before, you should totally dissolve your mind into the *short a* and thereby eliminate the gap between subject and object. When you are able to do this you will be able to ignite and cause the inner fire to blaze and thereby gain control over the winds so that they enter, abide and dissolve within the central channel. It is on the basis of this accomplishment that you will be able to generate the realization of mahamudra.

Igniting the flame of inner fire (22)

At this time the concentration that was generated in the fourth round of meditation is focussed in the vacuole of the navel channel-wheel. The object of meditation is the letter *short a* which is in the nature of fiery heat. You should now couple the previously described concentration with the holding of the vase breath.

Begin the vase breath by drawing a portion of the winds of the lower body upwards and gathering them just below the *short a* at the navel channel-wheel. This is accomplished by relying mainly on the power of imagination; merely feel that you are constricting the muscles of the lower part of your body and thereby drawing the winds gently upwards. In response, the muscles controlling the retention of urine and excrement, etc. from the two lower 'doors' will constrict slightly, but not to the extent that these two doors will actually close. Then inhale through both nostrils gently, slowly and deeply. Visualize that all the winds of the upper body flow down through the right and left channels. When they reach the navel they enter the central channel and gather just above the *short a*. The third part of this vase breath is actually to constrict the muscles of the pelvic floor so that they close the two lower doors and draw all the winds of the lower body completely up. These winds then unite with the winds already gathered just below the *short a*. Now gently swallow some saliva without making any noise. This presses the upper and lower winds together slightly.

Now think that the letter *short a* is completely enclosed by the upper and lower winds as if it were a jewel in an amulet box. (The size of this visualization is that of a small pea that has been cut in half, hollowed out and rejoined around an even smaller mustard seed.)

When this has been visualized, fix your attention single-pointedly on the small sphere and its enclosed syllable. Cease all inhalation and exhalation through the nostrils and do not let air enter or leave the mouth. Once you are concentrated in this way it is no longer necessary to keep the lower doors closed. Remain concentrated like this without breathing until you are about to become uncomfortable. Then, just before exhaling, visualize the upper and lower hemispheres of wind dissolving into the *short a* which, as a result, grows even hotter than before.

When you feel discomfort you can exhale slowly and gently through the nostrils (not from the mouth), all the while remaining concentrated upon the letter in the centre of the navel channel-wheel. Relax and then continue the vase breathing as before. You can take seven or twenty-one or more consecutive vase breaths in one meditation session depending upon the time you have available. If possible you should not take any additional breaths between the exhalation marking the end of one vase breath and the inhalation marking the beginning of the next. However, if this proves too difficult you may take a few intermediate breaths. (Note that while there are other ways of doing the vase breathing, they are not contradictory to the method just explained here. However, this particular vase breathing method is most suitable for the present practice.)

While doing this meditation do not let your concentration stray from its object, even momentarily. Always keep in mind that the *short a* is in the nature of fiery heat. Furthermore, you should repeat this practice of holding the vase breath frequently, as many times as you can, in order to become completely familiar with it.

It is very important that your concentration be accurately focussed upon the proper place within the central channel. The vacuole within the central channel is in the centre of the navel channel-wheel and it is here that the *short a* is visualized and the winds mingle. When doing this round of meditation there are four important tasks to keep in mind: (1) check constantly if the place of meditation is accurate, (2) find the object of meditation without difficulty, (3) hold the object of meditation continuously through the force of memory and (4) have your mind mix completely with the object of meditation.

On the basis of these four you will succeed not only in your meditation on inner fire but will also be able to cause the winds to enter, abide and dissolve within the central channel.

There are two purposes served by holding the vase breath. First, you arrest the flow of wind within the right and left channels and thereby pacify the gross conceptual minds. As stated before, when the winds stop flowing within the right and left channels they must flow within the central channel.

Concerning this first purpose it should be noted that it is possible to bring the winds into the central channel merely by concentrating upon the *short a*, without doing the vase breathing at all. This is the most 'peaceful' of all centralization techniques and it is excellent if you are able to do it. It will not incur the danger of possible disturbance of the winds and is more powerful than other techniques for gaining a realization of the clear light. However, by holding the vase breath you will be able to centralize the winds much more rapidly.

As indicated before the vase breathing technique itself can be performed either peacefully or violently. The technique described earlier wherein the muscles of the lower body doors are constricted gently is the recommended peaceful method. More violent is the method whereby the muscles of the arms and legs are also clenched, thereby forcing the lower winds up more rapidly. It is said that if a meditator does not experience success with a peaceful method, he or she should practise a more violent or wrathful one for a while and then return to the gentler technique.

There is a similarity between the different methods of centralizing the winds and the different ways of dying. The method whereby one merely concentrates on the *short a* is similar to the processes occurring during a natural death; in such a case the winds dissolve into the central channel slowly and progressively and therefore allow a greater opportunity for discerning and meditating upon the clear light. The most forceful vase breathing method is similar to what happens during a sudden, violent death. The winds dissolve very quickly and, as a result of this hurried movement, it is more difficult to be aware of the clear light experience. Therefore, the best way of meditating would be to use the vase breathing technique at first to gain experience in concentrating the mind on the *short a* in the navel channel-wheel and then, once familiarity has been established, proceed with the more peaceful method of using concentration alone.

The second purpose served by holding the vase breath has to do with the downward-voiding wind residing in the central channel just below the navel channel-wheel. By mixing the upper and lower winds of the body within the *short a* as described above, you will be able to move the downward-voiding wind upwards. When this happens the inner fire will ignite and blaze.

When people engage in sexual intercourse this downward-voiding wind is also caused to move upwards by the union of the male and female sex organs. However, this movement does not take place within the central channel and, as a result, the ordinary inner fire ignites and blazes only momentarily. Because of this ignition and blazing the drops in the lower part of the body melt and flow downwards. A brief experience of bliss is felt until the drops leave through the sex organ or, in the case of the woman, collect in the uterus.

By holding the vase breath and concentrating upon the inner fire, the downward-voiding wind can be caused to move upwards *inside* the central channel. Because of this upward movement the inner fire will ignite and blaze and the drops will melt—all *within* the central channel. Those not practising secret mantra cannot cause this to happen. Although through sexual intercourse they can ignite and cause the ordinary inner fire to blaze, they are unable to cause the drops to melt within the central channel nor can they cause them to descend all the way from the crown channel-wheel. The act of copulation cannot bring wind into the central channel nor cause the inner fire to ignite and blaze within it. Therefore, ordinary sexual intercourse can never benefit the practice of the completion stage.

Just as ordinary sexual intercourse can cause the inner fire to ignite and blaze in the fashion described, so too can certain ordinary meditations generate the heat of inner fire within the body. However, generating such heat serves no purpose other than keeping the body warm; it lacks the power to bring realizations. If your only aim is to warm the body, you do not need to do meditation; it would be easier simply to wrap yourself in an electric blanket or turn on the gas heater.

To practise inner fire purely you should strive to ignite the inner fire within the central channel. To ignite it outside this channel will only detract from the heat that could be generated within it. As a result the drops will not melt and flow within the central channel and the meditation will not bring any spiritual realizations of the completion stage. If the mahamudra meditation is not successful, it will not be possible to perceive the clear light. On the other hand, if the inner fire ignites and blazes *within* the central channel you will be able to cause the winds to enter, abide and dissolve within it as well. Then there will be nothing to prevent you from generating simultaneous great bliss: the main purpose of inner fire meditation.

Now you should endeavour to ignite the inner fire by means of the vase breath. Visualize that the dissolving of the upper and lower winds causes the downward-voiding wind to move upwards and blow against the *short a*. (Note that whereas before the lower winds of the body were merely visualized as ascending the central channel to form the lower half of the sphere surrounding the *short a*, now the downward-voiding wind below the navel channel-wheel actually does move upwards to blow against the letter.) Just as red coals grow hotter when blown upon by bellows, so does the *short a* burn more intensely now that the downward-voiding wind is fanning it. Visualize that the letter becomes so hot that it could consume anything. Its heat increases until it is on the verge of bursting into flame. Finally think that the finely tapered upper tip of the nada of the *short a* does begin to flame, after which it dies down again. The flame flares up and subsides again and again in the same way that coals do when

blown upon forcefully. This is called igniting the inner fire:
the fifth round of meditation. This practice should be con-
tinued until you have experienced this igniting.

According to the lineage of Je Tsong-khapa, each stage of
meditation should be done methodically and thoroughly, step
by step. If each stage is accomplished successfully the desired
result will surely follow. On the other hand, if you practise
inner fire meditation too quickly you may be able to generate
bodily heat but this will actually prove to be a hindrance to
receiving the true fruits of inner fire. Therefore, 'slowly but
surely' is the best attitude to adopt. Abandon all anxious
expectations, slow down and be thorough; then you will
achieve success. Many great meditators of the past took four,
five or six years to perfect the meditation on inner fire. You
can, in fact, spend an entire lifetime practising the yoga of
inner fire. As the Long-döl Lama said, 'Inner fire meditation
is like the wish-fulfilling cow from which you can receive an
inexhaustible supply of milk.'

Causing the inner fire to blaze (23)

The sixth round of meditation concerns the blazing of the
inner fire. This is very similar to the fifth round and is also
done in conjunction with the vase breathing meditation. As
always, the first step is to find the object of meditation. This is
the *short a* upon the moon cushion within the vacuole of the
central channel in the centre of the navel channel-wheel.
Remember that the *short a* is very red and in the nature of fire.
It is the size of a mustard seed and sparkles with radiant light.

After finding this object you should dissolve your mind
within it. If this is difficult you can think that the letter is your
body inside of which is your mind. Or you can think that the
short a is like clothes that you, the mind, are wearing. These
techniques will close the gap between the subjective mind and
the object of meditation.

Now practise the vase breathing, keeping your concentration firmly focussed upon the object of meditation. As before,
when the winds dissolve into the *short a* while you are holding

the vase breath, this causes the downward-voiding wind just below the navel channel-wheel to move upwards. This in turn causes the heat of the *short a* to increase powerfully. In the fifth round of meditation you visualized that the tapered upper end of the letter burst into flame and then died out again, and did so repeatedly. Now, however, the tapered upper end of the *short a* blazes constantly without dying down, just as coals in a fire, having been brought to life, blaze of their own accord.

The flame at the tip of the *short a* gradually increases in length until it is the size of a sewing needle, having the same diameter and being extremely sharp at its upper end. Though this flame is very small it is extremely powerful. Visualize this needle of flame in the exact centre of the central channel and standing very straight.

Next visualize that the powerful heat generated by this needle of fire ascends the central channel in the same way that heat rises from the tip of a candle flame. Warmed by this ascending heat the *huṁ*, *oṁ* and *haṁ* in the heart, throat and crown channel-wheels heat up until they are on the verge of melting.

At this time your concentration should be focussed primarily on the *short a* in the navel channel-wheel, but with a small portion of your mind you should visualize the other letters within the upper channel-wheels and feel that they are reaching the melting point. This entire visualization is done while holding the vase breath. Before it becomes uncomfortable to hold any longer, release the breath slowly and evenly through both nostrils. You should practise this meditation until you gain proficiency in it. As mentioned earlier, you can begin with vase breathing and then, when your concentration is well developed, continue the meditation with concentration alone.

When the fire blazes within the central channel as described, you will be able to generate simultaneous great bliss along with the melting of the white and red drops. When these melted drops flow within the central channel there will be no danger of losing them through the sex organ.

When you first start practising inner fire meditation you should emphasize the first round. When you gain some experience in that you should move to the second. Then move on to the third and so forth until you are proficient in all eight rounds. When you are skilled in the eight you can practise them all successively in one meditation session. In normal everyday life the time available for meditation is limited; therefore it may be difficult to devote enough time to each round to gain the desired proficiency. In this case, for the sake of gaining familiarity with the inner fire meditation you may practise all eight rounds in even one short sitting. However, this will not bring deep experience. It merely allows you to become familiar with all the technical methods of the eight rounds so that when you do have the time to practise thoroughly in retreat you will have a good idea of what you should do.

Blazing and dripping (24)

The seventh round is called 'blazing and dripping' and, as a further evolution of the sixth round, is also done in conjunction with the vase breathing. Again find the object of meditation—the *short a* and its needle of flame—and let the flame gradually grow longer. It is in the nature of very powerful fire and ascends the exact centre of the central channel. When it reaches the centre of the heart channel-wheel it coils clockwise once around the upside down letter *huṁ*, thereby bringing it closer to melting. Then the flame gradually continues up the central channel until it reaches the centre of the throat channel-wheel. Again it coils clockwise once around the letter there, the upright *oṁ*, bringing it closer to melting as well.

The thread of flame continues upwards until it reaches the centre of the crown channel-wheel and touches the bottom of the letter there. At this channel-wheel there is the white drop in the form of the upside down *haṁ*. When the flame touches it the white drop drips from the letter just as butter will melt and drip when it is held above the tongue of an open fire. At this point you can visualize the fire subsiding into the needle of flame of the *short a*. Note also that during this meditation there is no need to visualize the moon cushions beneath the letters.

The melted white drop drips from the *haṁ* in a long, fine thread, as thin as the thread of a spider's web. This is similar to the way honey drips in a long thread from a small hole punctured in a honey tin. As it drips down it dissolves into the *oṁ* at the throat, causing you to feel extremely blissful. Then it drips out of the *oṁ* until it reaches the heart channel-wheel. When it dissolves into the *huṁ* there, even more bliss is experienced than before. Lastly the drop reaches the navel channel-wheel and dissolves into the flame of the *short a*. This causes it to become even hotter in the same way that butter dripping onto an open fire will cause it to burn more intensely. As the heat of the letter increases, so does your experience of bliss. If possible, this entire visualization can be done while holding a vase breath. If this is too difficult, you may do the vase breathing beforehand and then, while breathing normally, increase the length of the needle of flame and continue with the rest of this round of meditation.

Extraordinary blazing and dripping (25)

Again, this eighth round is similar to the one before it and is also done in conjunction with the vase breathing. The needle of flame ascends the central channel somewhat like a red hot electric wire. It coils around the *huṁ* and *oṁ* as before and ascends to the centre of the crown channel-wheel. Once the flame reaches the *haṁ* the practice begins to differ from the preceding round. Instead of melting the white drop the thread of fire coils once clockwise around the letter, bringing it almost to the point of melting, and then continues through the central channel, arching downwards until it reaches the point where the central channel terminates between the eyebrows.

When the fire reaches the point between the eyebrows its light shines forth from this hole until it pervades the entire phenomenal universe, reaching instantly to the ends of space.

The three realms of desire, form and formlessness as well as the sentient beings who inhabit them are engulfed by this light of inner fire. The universe is like a vessel and the sentient beings inhabiting it are like its precious contents. The light of inner fire purifies the faults and defilements of this vessel and its contents and causes them to melt into light, mix together completely and become undifferentiated within a single small sphere of blue light. This sphere can be visualized before you, the size of a light bulb.

At this point you should visualize that all the enlightened buddhas of the three times and the ten directions[10] are embodied in the form of heroes and heroines: beings who achieved perfect buddhahood through the highest vajrayana practices. Beyond the sphere of light that you have already visualized, these heroes and heroines fill the space above and in front of you. They are sitting in the father/mother aspect of sublime single-pointed embrace. Now visualize that rays of brilliant blue light emanate forth from the sphere towards each divine couple and enter the left nostril of each father. This light then dissolves into the indestructible drop within each of their heart channel-wheels, thereby causing them to enter into the experience of uncontaminated simultaneous great bliss.

As each couple experiences this great bliss they melt into light. The father aspects melt into white drops and the mother into red. The drops deriving from each couple completely intermingle so that all that is left for each is a single white drop having a reddish tint and in the nature of great bliss. All these separate drops of light melt into one which comes and enters you at the point between your eyebrows. From here this powerful drop ascends your central channel until it reaches the letter *haṁ* in the centre of your crown channel-wheel. The drop then dissolves into the *haṁ* so that this letter becomes completely unified with all the enlightened beings in the essence of heroes and heroines. Feel that the *haṁ* has now become powerfully blessed by the power and wisdom of the buddhas of the three times and the ten directions. It is very important that your concentration on this be as single-pointed as possible.

Then turn your attention to the navel channel-wheel. As before, see the extremely hot fire generated by the *short a* as a needle of flame. Once again this powerful fire ascends the central channel, filling it and coming to the *haṁ* in the crown. (At this point to visualize the *huṁ* and the *oṁ* would be a distraction; therefore visualize the flame going straight up the central channel to the *haṁ*.) This flame causes the *haṁ* to melt and, as it does, the white drop begins to flow from it down the central channel until it reaches the *oṁ* in the throat channel-wheel. When the white drop touches the *oṁ*, this letter transforms until its nature is the synthesis of all the enlightened beings. After this the white drop flows down to the heart channel-wheel and touches the *huṁ* causing it to transform in the same way. And when this is accomplished the drop continues to flow down the central channel until it reaches the *short a* in the navel channel-wheel, transforming it as well. With great concentration you should feel that the *short a*, in the nature of great bliss, is the synthesis of all the enlightened beings of the three times and the ten directions.

This powerful blessing causes the heat generated by the *short a* to increase greatly. Remain in concentration for a while and then visualize that the blazing light of inner fire spreads throughout the sixty-four spokes of the navel channel-wheel. This light spreads throughout the 72,000 channels of the body, correcting all their defects and clarifying all the winds and drops. It also consumes all the negativities of body, speech and mind. The channels, winds and drops in this way become blessed by the power and wisdom of all the fully enlightened beings.

If you need to make your body warm through this meditation you should visualize that the light flowing within the 72,000 channels is very hot. However, if you lack skill such a visualization can detract from the heat in the central channel; this is not good at all and will prevent the proper fruit of inner fire meditation from ripening. There is even danger that your meditation on inner fire will degenerate into an impure dharma practice and thereby yield inferior results. As stated before in the section on the second round, the main objective of this meditation is to consecrate and bless all your channels, winds and drops, to purify all impure winds and annihilate every single gross and subtle negative thought including even the most subtle dualistic conceptualizing mind preventing your realization of perfect enlightenment. All these superior aims are accomplished through the experience of the light of inner fire.

Meditation on inner fire is a gradual process. If you experience much heat at the very beginning of your practice, this is probably an indication that your mind is not focussed on the proper place of meditation. Therefore, at the beginning heat should only be generated within the vacuole of the navel channel-wheel and in the central channel, not in the gross physical body.

In the Tibetan monastery of Se-gyu there was a great meditator by the name of Sang-gye Gyatso. His death occurred in the winter season when there was much snow on the ground. While he was passing away he remained in single-pointed meditation on clear light for one month. Because his concentration on the practice of inner fire was so powerful, all the snow around the monastery melted.

If you successfully consecrate and purify all your channels, winds and drops, your mind will naturally become extremely clear and lucid. As a result, you will receive certain limited supernatural powers, such as a degree of clairvoyance and foreknowledge. Predictions made by any meditator who reaches this level will be very accurate. All these powers are mere byproducts of meditating upon inner fire, yet even they are not the pure supernatural powers. As stated by the great Atisha in his *Lamp of the Path to Enlightenment*, one must have gained a thorough realization of tranquil abiding in order to gain the pure supernatural powers.

When the channels, winds and drops have been purified and the winds have been brought into the central channel, the dualistic conceptualizing mind—the source of all cyclic existence—will no longer have any foundation and will therefore disappear. Thus the myriad of negative thoughts powered by the dualistic view will all vanish automatically, without effort. As a result the mind will intuitively develop all positive qualities.

The eighth round of meditation is termed 'extraordinary' because it invokes the power and blessings of the heroes and heroines. This round of meditation contains three benefits: (1) it bestows the blessings of these heroes and heroines, (2) it consecrates and clarifies the channels, winds and drops and thereby destroys negative thoughts and (3) it causes the inner fire to ignite and blaze so that the drops will melt and flow within the central channel, giving rise to simultaneous great bliss.

This concludes the first section of the meditation on inner fire. This particular practice of inner fire is known as 'the fierce one having four wheels' and is principally explained in the *Hevajra Tantra* and also in the *Samputa Tantra* and *Little Samvara Tantra*. Most of the early yogis practised this system and achieved perfect realizations through it. Thus it is a most precious and invaluable treasure. The second section of this inner fire meditation now follows: the four joys and nine mixings.

3 Clear Light and the Four Joys

Based on these eight rounds, the experience of the four joys and the practice of the nine mixings (26)

As indicated by its title, this section of the outline is divided into two parts, explained in this and in the following chapter:

27 The development of the four joys
28 The practice of the nine mixings

The development of the four joys (27)

There are two sets of four joys: those of the generation stage and those of the completion stage. It is the latter that will be described here. Experiencing the four joys of the completion stage depends upon the winds entering, abiding and dissolving within the central channel. The method by which this is accomplished is the eight rounds of meditation upon the inner fire. If you practise these eight rounds successfully it is certain that you will be able to gain control over the winds in the manner desired.

It is very important to recognize when the winds have entered, abided and dissolved within the central channel. There are signs associated with each of these stages and it is with these signs that you must become intimately familiar. Therefore, before discussing the four joys it will be helpful to present an extensive description of these signs.

Manjushri

You can tell whether or not the winds have entered the central channel by checking your breathing. Normally there are imbalances in one's breath: more air is exhaled through one nostril than through the other and the breathing is not synchronized (the air begins to leave one nostril before the other). However, when the winds have entered the central channel as a result of the eight rounds of meditation, the pressure and the timing of the breath will be the same for both nostrils during inhalation and exhalation. Therefore, the first sign to be noticed is that you will be breathing evenly through both nostrils. Another noticeable imbalance in the normal breath is that the inhalation is stronger than the exhalation, or vice-versa. The second sign that the winds have indeed entered the central channel is that the pressure of the inhalation will be exactly equal to that of the exhalation.

The signs that the winds are abiding in the central channel are also two-fold: (1) your breathing will become weaker and weaker and will eventually cease completely and (2) all abdominal movement normally associated with the breath will stop. When these two signs appear they indicate that the winds are abiding within the central channel. In general, if you think your breathing has stopped you will be filled with panic believing that you are close to death. However, if you are able to stop breathing through the force of meditation, far from panicking your mind will become even more confident, comfortable and flexible.

When the winds are abiding within the central channel, you no longer have to rely upon gross air to survive. Normally your breathing stops only at the time of death. During sleep your breathing becomes much more subtle but it never stops completely. During completion stage meditation, however, your breath can come to a complete halt, without your becoming unconscious. After the winds have abided in the central channel for five or ten minutes, it is possible that they will again escape into the right and left channels. If this happens you will resume breathing. Whenever air is flowing through the nostrils it is an indication that the winds are not abiding within the central channel. When these winds *are* abiding there, there will be no respiration whatsoever.

As was the case with the winds entering and abiding in the central channel, there are also signs that these winds have dissolved within the central channel. There are seven winds that must dissolve and each has a specific sign indicating that its dissolution has been completed. The seven winds are:

(1) The earth element wind
(2) The water element wind
(3) The fire element wind
(4) The wind element wind
(5) The wind mounted by the mind of white appearance
(6) The wind mounted by the mind of red increase
(7) The wind mounted by the mind of black near-attainment

The first four of these winds are gross and the last three are subtle. These seven dissolve in a gradual step-by-step manner and with each dissolution a particular sign or vision will appear. As indicated before, meditation on inner fire not only causes the winds to enter and abide within the central channel but also causes them to dissolve there.

The *earth element wind* increases and supports everything that is associated with the earth element in your body, e.g. bones, cartilage, fingernails and so forth. When this wind dissolves within the central channel there occurs what is known as the *mirage-like appearance*. This is like the shimmering of an apparent lake that appears on hot, sunny days in the desert. There are three levels on which this mirage-like vision will be perceived depending upon the degree to which the earth element wind has dissolved into the central channel. If the dissolution is only slight the vision will be vague and not clear at all; such a sign will be very difficult to recognize. If the dissolution is almost complete the vision will be more clear and vivid. When the wind dissolves completely, the vision will be unmistakenly clear and vivid and impossible not to perceive. When the earth element dissolves and the vision has been perceived, the next vision will manifest as the next wind dissolves. The more completely the first wind dissolves the more it helps your perception of the subsequent vision.

The next wind to dissolve is the *water element wind* which increases and supports the liquid elements of the body, such as the blood and so forth. The vision associated with this dissolution is the so-called *smoke-like appearance*. Some texts state that this appearance is like the smoke that billows forth from a chimney but this is not the actual appearance. The vision of billowing smoke will in fact appear but it does so just prior to the actual dissolution of the water element wind. When this initial vision dissipates the actual smoke-like appearance will be perceived. This is like thin wisps of wafting blue smoke drifting in the air in a slowly swirling haze. As before, there are three levels on which this vision will appear depending upon the degree to which the water element wind has dissolved.

Next comes the dissolution of the *fire element wind*. This wind increases and supports the fire element in the body and is responsible for bodily heat and so forth. The sign that this wind has dissolved is the appearance of the *fireflies vision*. This vision is sometimes described in terms of an open crackling fire seen at night. The mass of ascending sparks swirling above such a fire is like the vision of fireflies. Once again, there are three levels on which this vision appears depending upon the degree of dissolution.

Following this the *wind element wind* dissolves. This is the wind mounted by gross conceptual thought. It powers gross dualistic appearances and the gross conceptual thoughts that result from holding these appearances to be true. The sign that the fourth of the gross winds has started to dissolve is the so-called *burning like a butter lamp appearance*. This is like the steady, erect flame of a dying butter lamp or candle in a draughtless room. And once again there are three levels on which this vision is perceived.

When the earth element wind has dissolved within the

central channel and the power of the earth element is thereby diminished, it may seem as though the water element has increased. As the power of the former diminishes, the latter is perceived more clearly. For this reason the dissolution of the earth element wind into the central channel is often described as the earth element dissolving into the water element. For similar reasons the subsequent dissolutions are referred to as the water element dissolving into the fire element, the fire element dissolving into the wind element and the wind element dissolving into consciousness.

After the appearance of the butter lamp vision, all the gross conceptual minds cease functioning because the winds they are mounted upon have dissolved and disappeared. When the meditator has completed the dissolution of the fourth wind, the first subtle mind—the *mind of white appearance*—is generated. As before there are three levels of clarity to the vision depending on the ability of the meditator.

When the mind of white appearance arises the meditator perceives the vision of whiteness. At this point the mind has no gross conceptualizations, such as the eighty indicative conceptions listed below. The vision is like that of an empty sky on a clear autumn night pervaded by the bright light of the full moon. The only perception that occurs is of this white empty space. Ordinary beings perceive this vision at the time of their death but are unable to recognize and prolong it. Why is this? At the time of this dissolution, the ordinary gross level of mindfulness has ceased to function. This is true for both greatly accomplished meditators and ordinary beings. However, those who have trained properly according to the practices of secret mantra are able to take advantage of the *subtle* level of mindfulness developed during meditation. It is with this subtle mindfulness that they are able to recognize and prolong the vision of white appearance, something ordinary beings are unable to do.

When the subtle wind mounted by the mind of white appearance dissolves, the *mind of red increase* will arise. This mind and its wind are more subtle than the mind and wind of the white appearance. The sign that appears with the arisal of this mind is the vision of an empty sky pervaded by sunlight.

When the subtle wind mounted by the mind of red increase dissolves, the *mind of black near-attainment* will arise. Again, this subtle mind and its mounted wind are even more subtle than the mind and wind of red increase. The mind of black near-attainment has two levels: the so-called upper and lower parts. The upper part of the mind of black near-attainment still possesses subtle mindfulness or memory while the lower part has no mindfulness or memory whatsoever and is experienced as an overwhelming unconsciousness like that of a very deep faint. When this is experienced you will appear to others as if you were actually dead.

The appearance associated with the mind of black near-attainment is that of a very black empty sky. This appearance occurs with the upper part of the mind of black near-attainment, immediately after the cessation of the mind of red increase. As the experience of black near-attainment progresses and you approach complete unconsciousness, your subtle mindfulness ceases. The more forcefully the wind dissolves into the central channel, the more unconscious you become during the appearance of black near-attainment. And the more unconscious you become at this time, the more vividly you will perceive the subsequent appearance of clear light. This is similar to the experience of a man who stays in a dark room for a long time. The longer he stays there, the brighter the outside world will appear when he eventually leaves the room. The degree of brightness experienced is proportionate to the depth and duration of the previous darkness.

After the appearance of the mind of black near-attainment, the subtle mindfulness will be restored according to the meditator's development. It is with the re-emergence of this subtle mindfulness that the *clear light* will appear. This appearance is like that of an autumn sky at dawn: perfectly clear and empty.

The mindfulness that emerges during the clear light is

extremely subtle. The very subtle wind and the very subtle mind that is mounted upon it reside in the indestructible drop in the centre of the heart channel-wheel. Normally, the very subtle mind is not functioning. At the time of the clear light, however, it awakens and becomes active. If you have trained in the techniques of secret mantra yoga and have become proficient in them, you will be able to perceive and maintain the experience of clear light consciously. Because of the extremely subtle mindfulness developed through meditation, you will be able to turn your mind to emptiness at this time of clear light. By doing this you will be able to take this mind of clear light as the means of attaining a buddha's truth body (dharmakaya).

Your mind cannot become more subtle than the mind of clear light. During the first four appearances—mirage, smoke, fireflies and butter lamp—the gross winds dissolve. And from the initial arisal of the mind of white appearance to the end of the mind of black near-attainment the subtle winds dissolve. At the appearance of the clear light the very subtle mind and its mounted wind awaken and become active. They themselves cannot dissolve because they are indestructible. After death they simply move on to the next life.

Concerning the three subtle winds—those of white appearance, red increase and black near-attainment—the most gross of these is the one mounted by the mind of white appearance. It is called 'white appearance' because there is no object of perception other than that of an empty white sky. It is also termed 'empty' because the mind of white appearance perceives this white sky as empty.

When the wind mounted by the mind of white appearance dissolves, the second of the three subtle minds arises, that of red increase. The mounting wind of this mind is more subtle than that mounted by the mind of white appearance. It is called 'red increase' because the appearance of the red sky is increasing. It is also called 'very empty' because the appearance of being empty is stronger here than during the previous sign. (It should be noted that during the first sign the appearance of being white and the appearance of being empty are of equal strength. During the second, however, the appearance of being empty is stronger than the appearance of being red.)

When the wind of the mind of red increase dissolves the mind of black near-attainment will arise. It is called 'near attainment' because the experience of clear light is now close at hand. Furthermore, because the appearance of being empty is greater than that of the second sign it is also called 'great empty'.

When the third subtle wind, that mounted by the mind of black near-attainment, dissolves the clear light appears. It is called 'clear light' because its nature is very lucid and clear and because it is perceived as the light of an autumn dawn. It is also known as 'all empty' because it is empty of all gross and subtle winds; the only appearance perceived by it is that of being empty. The object of the mind of clear light is very similar in appearance to what is perceived by the equipoise wisdom of an arya meditator in single-pointed concentration upon emptiness.

If the secret mantra meditator is highly accomplished, he or she will have a very vivid experience of clear light and be able to abide in that experience for an extended time. Having such a vivid experience depends on how vivid the previous seven appearances have been. And this depends on how forcefully the winds have dissolved within the central channel. If they dissolve very forcefully, you will have a vivid experience of the appearances and you will be able to prolong the experience of each one. The longer you are able to remain in each appearance the longer you will be able to spend in the clear light itself. When a person dies a violent death, he or she progresses through these appearances very rapidly. If the death is a slow or natural one the appearances will be experienced longer and more gradually. Furthermore, if you have developed the realization of the isolated mind of the completion stage—as will be explained in more detail later—then you will be able to have exactly the same experience of these appearances while in deep concentration that you would have if you were actually dying. If you have trained in meditation you will

be able to meditate upon emptiness—that is upon the emptiness of inherent existence—throughout all four empties except
during the time spent in the swoon or faint of the mind of
black near-attainment.

To be able to perceive the four empties clearly, exactly as in
the death process, you must be able to dissolve all the winds
into the indestructible drop of the heart channel-wheel. If they
dissolve in another channel-wheel you will experience similar,
but artificial appearances. They will not be the true appearances that occur when the winds dissolve in the indestructible
drop as they do at the actual time of death.

Although as an accomplished meditator you can abide
within the clear light for an extended time, you still must
move on eventually. When you arise from the appearance of
clear light the first thing you will experience is the mind of
black near-attainment of reverse order. Then comes the mind
of red increase, the mind of white appearance, the eighty gross
conceptual minds and so forth in an order that is the reverse of
the sequence in which the winds originally dissolved. The
mind of clear light is the foundation of all other minds. When
the gross and subtle minds and mounted winds dissolve into
the indestructible drop at the heart, you perceive only the
clear light and it is from this clear light that all other minds—
each one more gross than the one it follows—are regenerated.

It is generally stated that there are twenty-five gross phenomena that dissolve when a sentient being moves through the
process of death. These gross phenomena are:

The five aggregates
    (1) the aggregate of form
    (2) the aggregate of feeling
    (3) the aggregate of discernment
    (4) the aggregate of compositional factors
    (5) the aggregate of consciousness

The four elements
    (6) the earth element
    (7) the water element

(8) the fire element
(9) the wind element

The six sense faculties
(10) the sense faculty of the eye
(11) the sense faculty of the ear
(12) the sense faculty of the nose
(13) the sense faculty of the tongue
(14) the sense faculty of the body
(15) the sense faculty of the mind

The five objects
(16) the forms included within one's own continuum
(17) the sounds included within one's own continuum
(18) the smells included within one's own continuum
(19) the tastes included within one's own continuum
(20) the tactile sensations included within one's own continuum

The five basic wisdoms
(21) the basic mirror-like wisdom
(22) the basic wisdom of equality
(23) the basic wisdom of individual analysis
(24) the basic wisdom of accomplishing activities
(25) the basic wisdom of dharmadhatu

The first four of these groups are easily understood. As for the five basic wisdoms, a brief explanation of them follows. The basic mirror-like wisdom is so called because just as a mirror can simultaneously reflect many objects of various forms so too can one ordinary mind perceive many objects simultaneously. The mind that remembers experiences as having been pleasurable, painful and neutral is the basic wisdom of equality. The basic wisdom of individual analysis remembers individual names of one's friends and relatives and so forth. A mind that remembers normal external activities,

purposes and so forth is the basic wisdom of accomplishing
activities. And the fifth, the basic wisdom of dharmadhatu, is
the mind that is the seed of the wisdom truth body of a buddha.

At the time of death most people experience the dissolution of
these twenty-five objects in the order indicated below with certain phenomena dissolving in relation to each of the five aggregates as follows:

The five phenomena on the level of the form aggregate
    (1) the aggregate of form
    (2) the basic mirror-like wisdom
    (3) the earth element
    (4) the sense faculty of the eye
    (5) the forms included within one's own
        continuum

The five phenomena on the level of the feeling aggregate
    (6) the aggregate of feeling
    (7) the basic wisdom of equality
    (8) the water element
    (9) the sense faculty of the ear
  (10) the sounds included within one's own
        continuum

The five phenomena on the level of the discernment aggregate
  (11) the aggregate of discernment
  (12) the basic wisdom of individual analysis
  (13) the fire element
  (14) the sense faculty of the nose
  (15) the smells included within one's own
        continuum

The five phenomena on the level of the compositional factors
aggregate
  (16) the aggregate of compositional factors
  (17) the basic wisdom of accomplishing activities
  (18) the wind element
  (19) the sense faculty of the tongue
  (20) the tastes included within one's own
        continuum

The five phenomena on the level of the consciousness aggregate
  (21) the eighty indicative conceptions
  (22) the mind of white appearance
  (23) the mind of red increase
  (24) the mind of black near-attainment
  (25) the mind of the clear light of death

The external signs associated with each of the five phenomena on the level of the form aggregate are:

  (1) the limbs of the body become thinner and the
      body becomes weak and loses its power
  (2) one's vision becomes unclear and blurred
  (3) the body becomes thin, the limbs loose and
      one has the feeling of sinking underground
  (4) one can no longer open or close one's eyes
  (5) the lustrous complexion of the body is lost and
      one's beauty diminishes

The internal sign associated with these five dissolutions is the mirage-like appearance. What does it look like? When seen from a distance the sunshine on the floor of a desert will look like water. The mirage-like appearance is similar and arises because the wind of the earth element has dissolved within the central channel. As the power of the earth element decreases it seems that the power of the water element becomes clearer; thus one perceives the appearance of water in a shimmering mirage-like vision.

The external signs associated with each of the five phenomena on the level of the feeling aggregate are:

  (6) the bodily consciousness no longer experiences
      pleasant, unpleasant or indifferent feelings
  (7) one no longer individually experiences the
      feelings of mental peace, mental suffering or
      mental indifference
  (8) the liquids of the body begin to dry up
  (9) one no longer perceives external sounds
  (10) the inner sound of the whirring in the ears is
      no longer perceived

The internal sign associated with these five dissolutions is the smoke-like appearance. This is the sign that the water element is losing power and that the fire element is apparently becoming clearer.

The external signs associated with each of the five phenomena on the level of the discernment aggregate are:

(11) one can no longer recognize close relatives and friends

(12) one can no longer remember the names of close relatives and friends

(13) the heat leaves the body and the digestion stops

(14) one's inhalation becomes weak and shallow while the exhalation becomes long and strong; one begins to wheeze and make the sound of the death rattle

(15) one can no longer detect smells and one's own odour

The internal sign associated with these five dissolutions is the fireflies or sparks appearance. This is due to the increased clarity of the wind element.

The external signs associated with each of the five phenomena on the level of the compositional factors aggregate are:

(16) one can no longer move

(17) one can no longer remember the purpose for work and activities or even what they were during the life-time now ending

(18) there is no longer any inhalation and exhalation from the nostrils; all the breathing stops now that the ten winds have gathered at the heart

(19) the tongue becomes short and thick and blue at its root and one can no longer speak clearly

(20) one can no longer experience tastes

Also, at this time the body can no longer experience any
sensation of pleasure, pain or indifference nor the sensations
of roughness and smoothness, hardness and softness, heat and
cold and so forth. This is due to the dissolution of the sense
faculty of the body and the tactile sensations included within
one's own continuum. The internal sign associated with all of
these dissolutions is the butter lamp appearance.

Up until now most of the gross minds and their winds have
dissolved; what remains is the experience of the dissolutions of
the aggregate of consciousness. The consciousness aggregate
has gross and subtle levels. The last gross mind to dissolve is
necessarily one of (21) the eighty indicative conceptions.
(Which one of these it is depends on the dying person's
activities and habits of this life. For example, if he or she had
trained extensively in bodhicitta the last gross mind to arise
could well be that of compassion. On the other hand, the last
gross conception in the continuum of someone with an unruly
mind might well be anger, attachment or the like.) Now that
the butter lamp vision has appeared, the last of these eighty
minds arises. Along with this last gross mind of the consciousness aggregate, the sense faculty of the mind and the
basic wisdom of dharmadhatu also absorb.

The eighty gross conceptions are divided into three groups:
thirty-three indicative of the mind of white appearance, forty
indicative of the mind of red increase and seven indicative of
the mind of black near-attainment. The meaning of 'indicative' can be understood by considering the first group.[11] These
thirty-three conceptions involve a coarse movement to their
objects of the winds serving as their mounts. Thus they help
indicate, for those who have not obviously experienced the
mind of white appearance, that the wind serving as the mount
of this mind of white appearance has a somewhat coarse
movement when compared with the winds of the other two
subtle minds. This inference about the mind of white
appearance can be drawn because the first group of conceptions is an imprint or effect of the mind of white appearance
when proceeding in reverse order from the subtler to the

grosser states. In a similar fashion, the second and third groups involve a middling and a weak movement respectively of their mounted winds, thereby serving to indicate the same with regard to the winds of red increase and black near-attainment. These three groups of gross conceptions are listed as follows:

The thirty-three conceptions indicative of the mind of white appearance

  (1) great separation from attachment: a mind not desiring an object
  (2) middling separation from attachment
  (3) small separation from attachment
  (4) mental going and coming: a mind going to external objects and coming to internal ones
  (5) great sorrow: the mental anxiety experienced upon separation from an attractive object
  (6) middling sorrow
  (7) small sorrow
  (8) peace: a mind remaining peacefully
  (9) conceptuality: a mind distracted towards an external object
 (10) great fear: the mind of fright generated upon meeting an unpleasant object
 (11) middling fear
 (12) small fear
 (13) great craving: a mind attracted to a pleasant object
 (14) middling craving
 (15) small craving
 (16) grasping: a mind thoroughly holding to objects of desired enjoyment
 (17) non-virtue: doubt with respect to virtuous actions
 (18) hunger: a mind desiring food
 (19) thirst: a mind desiring drink
 (20) great feeling: feelings of pleasure, pain and neutrality

(21) middling feeling

(22) small feeling

(23) conception of a cognizer

(24) conception of cognizing

(25) conception of an object cognized

(26) individual investigation: a mind investigating what is suitable and unsuitable

(27) shame: abandoning misconduct because of one's own disapproval or religious convictions

(28) compassion: a mind wishing for separation from suffering

(29) mercy: a mind thoroughly protecting an object of observation

(30) desire to meet the beautiful

(31) qualm: a captivated mind, one not abiding in certainty

(32) collection: a mind of gathering possessions

(33) jealousy: a mind disturbed by others' good fortune and excellent qualities

The forty conceptions indicative of the mind of red increase

(1) attachment: a mind attached to an object not yet attained

(2) adherence: a mind attached to an object already attained

(3) great joy: a joyous mind upon seeing what is attractive

(4) middling joy

(5) small joy

(6) rejoicing: a happy mind from having achieved a desired object

(7) rapture: a mind repeatedly experiencing a desired object

(8) amazement: contemplating an object that did not arise before

(9) excitement: a mind distracted through perceiving an attractive object

(10) contentment: a mind satisfied with a pleasant object
(11) embracing: a mind wishing to embrace
(12) kissing: a mind wishing to kiss
(13) sucking: a mind wishing to suck
(14) stability: a mind of unchanging continuum
(15) effort: a mind tending towards virtue
(16) pride: a mind of considering oneself high
(17) activity: a mind of completing an activity
(18) robbery: a mind wishing to rob wealth
(19) force: a mind wishing to conquer others' troops
(20) delight: a mind becoming accustomed to the path of virtue
(21) the great innate born: a mind engaging in non-virtue because of arrogance
(22) the middling innate born
(23) the small innate born
(24) vehemence: wishing to debate with the excellent for no reason
(25) flirtation: desiring to play upon seeing the attractive
(26) angry disposition: a mind of resentment
(27) virtue: a mind desiring to make an effort at virtuous actions
(28) clear word and truth: a mind wishing to speak so that others can understand; a mind that does not change its discernment of the facts
(29) untruth: a mind wishing to speak having changed one's discernment of the facts
(30) definiteness: a mind of very steady intent
(31) non-grasping: a mind not desiring to hold an object
(32) donor: a mind wishing to give away possessions
(33) exhortation: a mind wishing to exhort the lazy to practise the dharma

(34) heroism: a mind wishing to overcome enemies such as the delusions

(35) non-shame: a mind engaging in non-virtue, not abandoning misconduct despite one's own disapproval or religious prohibitions

(36) pretension: a mind deceiving others through hypocrisy

(37) tightness: a mind of sharp conscientiousness

(38) badness: a mind used to a bad view

(39) non-gentleness: a mind desiring to injure others

(40) dishonesty: a mind of crookedness

The seven conceptions indicative of the mind of black near-attainment

(1) middling attachment: a mind of equal attachment and hatred

(2) forgetfulness: a mind of degenerated memory or mindfulness

(3) mistake: a mind that apprehends water in a mirage and so forth

(4) non-speaking: a mind not wishing to speak

(5) depression: a mind of annoyance

(6) laziness: a mind having displeasure in virtue

(7) doubt: a mind of uncertainty

From this point onwards the dying person will experience the dissolution of the subtle minds. As stated, (22) the mind of white appearance perceives what looks like a clear empty sky pervaded by a bright white light. This appearance arises because the knot in the crown channel-wheel has completely opened, releasing the white drop which then descends through the central channel. This bright white light appears while the drop is descending towards the heart channel-wheel and lasts until it reaches the top of the indestructible drop. Thus the actual object of perception at this time is like a vision of the empty sky, but this vision is pervaded by whiteness because of the descending white drop. This perceptual mind is variously called 'the white appearance', 'empty' or 'the first empty'.

When the descending white drop and its wind finally dissolve into the indestructible drop at the heart, the sign of their dissolution is the appearance of (23) the mind of red increase. This appearance is due to the untying of the knot of the navel channel-wheel which releases the red drop, freeing it to ascend the central channel. As it ascends and until it reaches the bottom of the indestructible drop, the dying person perceives the appearance of the mind of red increase. This perceptual mind is variously called 'red increase', 'very empty' or 'the second empty'.

At this point the indestructible drop is completely enclosed within the two drops: the white which descended from the crown and the red which ascended from the navel. These two drops cover the indestructible drop like a box. Just as the joining of the upper and lower halves of a box produces utter darkness inside, so too is there an experience of darkness here. The mind perceiving this darkness is (24) the mind of black near-attainment and what appears to it is perceived as an empty sky pervaded by black light. This is experienced when the mind of red increase and its mounted wind have dissolved into the indestructible drop. As stated before, when the mind of black near-attainment first appears the dying person retains subtle memory or mindfulness, but as this appearance progresses one loses all memory entirely. This perceptual mind is variously called 'the black near-attainment', 'the great empty' or 'the third empty'.

After the experience of the mind of black near-attainment, the two drops separate because the knots of the heart channel-wheel have become completely untied. When this happens the white drop continues downwards and the red upwards and the dying person experiences (25) the mind of the clear light of death, which is a vision of a clear, empty sky at dawn. In the same way that slowly removing the lid of a box exposes more and more light inside, the separation of the two enclosing drops results in the experience of the clear light. As the drops separate the dying person regains a very subtle mindfulness as a result of the awakening of the very subtle mind and its mounted wind. This perceptual mind is variously called 'the clear light of death', 'the all empty' or 'the fourth empty'.

As long as one is experiencing the clear light of death, one is not actually dead yet. The indestructible drop at the heart—present throughout life and formed from the very subtle white and red drops received from one's parents at conception—has not yet opened. When it does the very subtle mind and its mounted wind are free to travel to the next life.

During the experience of the clear light all the winds dissolve into the indestructible drop at the heart. After this process is completed, the very subtle white and red drops constituting the indestructible drop finally do separate and the movement of the very subtle mind and its mounted wind to the next life can then take place. The general external sign that one has actually died and that the very subtle mind and wind have departed is the exiting of the white drop from the sex organ and the red drop from the nostrils. These signs do not occur, however, for those who die a sudden or violent death.

When the experience of clear light ceases, the profound swoon of the mind of black near-attainment of the intermediate state will arise. Then, as mentioned above, one experiences the mind of red increase, then the mind of white appearance, then the re-emergence of the eighty indicative conceptions and the butter lamp vision, followed by the fireflies, the smoke and finally the mirage-like appearance along with their associated consciousnesses. Thus, after the clear light of death the intermediate state being experiences the remaining seven signs of death in reverse order.

If within seven days the intermediate state being has not found karmically appropriate conditions in which to take rebirth, that being will experience a small death and afterwards take another intermediate state body. The eight signs—from mirage to clear light—are experienced when one intermediate state life comes to an end and the seven signs of the reverse order—from black near-attainment to mirage—are experienced when the next intermediate state life begins.

After a maximum of forty-nine days in the intermediate state, the being will definitely find an appropriate place of rebirth. When this place becomes available, the intermediate state being will die and perceive the eight signs from the mirage to the clear light. Then, taking the example of a being who has the karma to be reborn a human, when the clear light experience comes to an end, the very subtle mind and its mounted wind will take rebirth in a human mother's womb during conception. The first mind of conception in the womb is that of black near-attainment after which the remaining signs of the reverse order are gradually experienced. Along with the differentiation and development of the foetus, the mind of the newly conceived being becomes grosser and grosser.

This has been a very brief explanation of death, intermediate state and rebirth but it is sufficient for an understanding of the process that must be controlled and transformed by the practitioner of secret mantra mahamudra.[12]

Thus far in this text the term 'clear light' has often appeared and it has been used to refer to several different types of experience. Because the experience of clear light is of central importance in mahamudra meditation it will be beneficial to discuss, at least in a general manner, the meaning of the different technical terms pertaining to this phenomenon.

Clear light can be defined as 'the very subtle mind that arises through the force of the mind of black near-attainment and is experienced directly after this mind of black near-attainment has ceased.' Therefore, the clear light at death, for example, can only be experienced after the cessation of the seventh sign of dying. There are two categories into which the experience of the clear light can be divided: the mother clear light and the son clear light. The former refers to the clear light that arises naturally during sleep and death. The latter only arises when the winds have dissolved within the central channel through the force of meditation.

The son clear light can be divided in two different ways. One way of dividing it is into the isolated and the non-isolated minds of clear light. The term 'isolated mind' in general refers to a mind that is isolated from the winds upon which the gross minds are mounted. Thus it can be used in respect to any of the four empties that arise when, through the force of meditation, the winds dissolve within the indestructible drop at the heart channel-wheel. Therefore, the mind of radiant white appearance that arises through the force of the dissolution of the winds within the indestructible drop of the heart by means of meditation is an isolated mind but is not the isolated mind of clear light. The same is true for the minds of red increase and black near-attainment. Only the mind that develops after the isolated mind of black near-attainment, which is the fourth empty, is in fact the isolated mind of clear light.

As for the non-isolated mind of clear light, this is the clear light that arises when, through meditation, the winds dissolve into the central channel through any of the nine doors other than the heart channel-wheel. As before, such a mind can be experienced only after the mind of black near-attainment, but not that mind of black near-attainment that arises when the winds dissolve within the central channel via the heart. (It should be noted that the non-isolated mind is, in fact, isolated in terms of its being removed from the gross winds as well.)

The son clear light can also be divided into the example, or metaphoric, clear light and meaning clear light. When the son clear light realises emptiness conceptually—i.e. through a mental image—it is example clear light. On the other hand, if the son clear light realizes emptiness intuitively or directly—without a mental image—then it is known as the meaning clear light.

The example clear light also has two divisions: the isolated mind of example clear light and the non-isolated mind of example clear light. When the son clear light realizes emptiness via a mental image due to the winds dissolving in the central channel but not at the indestructible drop at the heart, this is non-isolated example clear light. The isolated mind of example clear light arises when the son clear light, which has arisen due to the winds dissolving within the indestructible drop at the heart, realizes emptiness via a mental image.

And again, the isolated mind of example clear light has two divisions: the isolated mind of ultimate and non-ultimate example clear light. The isolated mind of ultimate, or final, example clear light is the clear light that arises through the force of dissolving all the winds including the entire pervading wind into the indestructible drop at the heart. The isolated mind of the non-ultimate example clear light is the clear light that arises through the force of dissolving any of the winds other than the entire pervading wind, even partially, into the indestructible drop. The experience of both the ultimate and non-ultimate example clear light depends on the knots of the heart channel-wheel being loosened. This is because both the ultimate and non-ultimate example clear lights are isolated minds. The methods for attaining these isolated minds is explained in the five stages of the completion stage (see chapter 8).

It is possible to loosen the knots of the heart channel-wheel completely through such meditations as the vajra recitation of the *Guhyasamaja Tantra,* inner fire and so forth. (Although the eight rounds of inner fire meditation described earlier focus primarily on the navel channel-wheel, once the central channel has been penetrated through any door it is relatively easy to proceed with loosening the knots at the heart.) However, after all the knots of the heart have been loosened through meditation, meditation alone is not enough to cause all the pervading winds of the body to dissolve into the indestructible drop before death. Therefore, when the power of such techniques as the vajra recitation and the inner fire has been completed, there comes the time when the secret mantra practitioner must either accept an action seal or wait until the clear light of death as explained below. Without accepting such an action seal there is no way before death that meditation alone can cause the dissolution of all the pervading winds into the indestructible drop at the heart and the achievement of the ultimate example clear light. The fully qualified secret mantra practitioner who does not accept an action seal can experience the isolated mind of ultimate example clear light during the experience of the clear light of death. This will be explained in more detail in section 89.

Once the isolated mind of ultimate example clear light has been attained before death, it is definite that the meditator will achieve enlightenment in that lifetime. When such a meditator emerges from the session in which the isolated mind of the ultimate example clear light is attained, he or she will automatically attain the impure illusory body. It is termed 'impure' because the practitioner has not yet abandoned the obscurations preventing liberation. This is so because the arya paths, achieved in secret mantra when emptiness has been realized intuitively by the mind of simultaneous great bliss, have not yet been attained. When this yogi has achieved the impure illusory body and meditates upon emptiness continuously, he or she will eventually achieve the spiritual path of the secret mantra arya and at the same time achieve the meaning clear light. When this meditator emerges from the meditative equipoise of meaning clear light he or she will automatically attain the pure illusory body which becomes the holy form body (rupakaya) of a fully enlightened buddha. In this way, then, is enlightenment assured for the meditator who has attained the isolated mind of ultimate example clear light before death.

According to secret mantra the eighth sign, the clear light of death, is the basic truth body. The intermediate state body that follows is called the basic enjoyment body and the body in which rebirth is taken is called the basic emanation body. These three are not the actual truth, enjoyment and emanation bodies of a buddha; they are merely the bases of purification. They serve as these bases in both the generation and completion stages of secret mantra practice.

In completion stage meditation these three basic bodies are

purified directly. The ordinary clear light of death is purified through the force of the isolated mind of ultimate example clear light. When this isolated mind meditates upon emptiness, which is like pouring water into water, it becomes the mahamudra that is the union of bliss and emptiness. By experiencing the great bliss nature of clear light and meditating upon emptiness with this isolated mind, the meditator will avoid experiencing ordinary death. And because he or she has purified the clear light of death in this way, the meditator will also avoid experiencing the ordinary intermediate state—whose mind and body have as their substantial cause the ordinary clear light of death and its associated wind—and instead will achieve the illusory body. The isolated mind of ultimate example clear light becomes the mind of the illusory body and the wind upon which it is mounted becomes the illusory body itself.

The meditator who can purify the ordinary clear light of death and the ordinary intermediate state in this way will naturally be able to purify ordinary rebirth as well and transform it into the spiritual path. The key to purifying these three bases is the attainment of the isolated mind of ultimate example clear light. This isolated mind is like the alchemical elixir that can change base metals into gold in that it transforms ordinary death, intermediate state and rebirth into the three holy bodies of a fully enlightened buddha.

In both the generation and completion stages of secret mantra it is important to have a clear understanding of three things: (1) the bases of purification, (2) that which purifies these bases and (3) the results or fruit of this purification. The bases of purification are the same in both stages of secret mantra meditation but that which purifies them is different. It has already been mentioned that in the completion stage the ordinary clear light of death is purified directly by the isolated mind of ultimate example clear light, the ordinary intermediate state by the illusory body and the ordinary rebirth by the yoga of the emanation body, which follows attainment of the illusory body. In generation stage practices these three ordinary bases are purified by the three yogas known as taking the three bodies into the path. These three yogas purify their bases indirectly and thus the generation stage practices are like a rehearsal for the actual purifications that take place on the completion stage. If your generation stage meditations are successful, those of the completion stage will also be very powerful. And when these latter are successful the three bases can be purified without much difficulty and you will attain the three resultant purified bodies—the actual truth body, enjoyment body and emanation body—and will thereby achieve complete buddhahood.

Now that the discussion of the ways in which the winds enter, abide and dissolve within the central channel has been completed it is possible to proceed with an explanation of the method by which the four joys are produced through the practice of inner fire.

By meditating for a sustained period of time upon the *short a* within the centre of the navel channel-wheel and by mixing your mind thoroughly with this object of meditation, you will be able to cause the winds to enter, abide and dissolve within the central channel as described. As these winds enter the door of the navel channel-wheel the downward-voiding wind—located just below this channel-wheel—will be caused to move upwards. This in turn will ignite the inner fire—visualized as the letter *short a*—and cause it to blaze. The heat generated in this fashion will melt the white drop in the crown channel-wheel—visualized as the upside down letter *haṁ*—and it will begin to flow downwards through the central channel. It is this movement of the white drop gently down the central channel that gives rise to the experience of joy or bliss.

When this drop reaches the centre of the throat channel-wheel you experience the first joy, simply called 'joy'. By stabilizing your meditative concentration upon the *oṁ* visualized in the throat centre you will be able to experience this first joy for a prolonged period of time. This first stage of joy will be experienced for as long as the white drop does not flow past the throat channel-wheel.

After remaining for a time in this channel-wheel the white drop should be allowed to continue down the central channel. When it reaches the centre of the heart channel-wheel you will experience the second of the four joys, known as 'supreme joy' because the bliss experienced at this time is greater than the first joy. Again, you will be able to maintain this blissful experience by concentrating on the letter *hum* in the heart centre.

After remaining in supreme joy for a while you should allow the white drop to flow down to the centre of the navel channel-wheel. When this happens you will experience the third and even greater joy, known as 'extraordinary joy'. If your meditation upon inner fire has been successful, you will be able to maintain this experience of extraordinary joy for as long as you wish.

Next the white drop flows down from the navel channel-wheel until it reaches the tip of the sex organ. This gives rise to the fourth of the four joys, known as 'simultaneous joy', which is a stage of simultaneous great bliss. This blissful experience is superior to the three preceding joys and can be maintained for a long time. In ordinary beings, when the white drop reaches the tip of the sex organ it is soon released and the strength of the blissful experience quickly diminishes. For an accomplished secret mantra meditator, however, this does not happen. Because the yogi has caused the winds to enter, abide and dissolve within the central channel and has gained control over the downward-voiding wind, the white drop will flow only within the central channel and thus can be held at the tip of the sex organ without being released.

When you have gained this blissful experience you should use the mind of simultaneous joy to meditate upon the emptiness of inherent existence. After remaining in this experience for a time you should reverse the flow of the white drop and cause it to move upwards through the central channel. Before becoming accustomed to this meditation, you will need to use a great deal of concentration to accomplish this reversal. With practice, however, you will be able to reverse the flow of the white drop quite naturally and with little effort.

As the white drop flows upwards you will again have the experience of four increasingly powerful states of joy. Because the white drop is now flowing upwards, these are called the four joys of the reverse order. Each of these is a stage of simultaneous great bliss and should be experienced in conjunction with voidness meditation.

The first 'joy' of the reverse order arises when the white drop reaches the navel channel-wheel. When it reaches the heart you will experience the 'supreme joy' of the reverse order and when it arrives at the throat you will experience 'extraordinary joy'. Finally, when the white drop reaches the centre of the crown channel-wheel you will experience the 'simultaneous joy' of the reverse order. This is the highest of all the experiences of joy. When it occurs you will be pervaded by tremendous bliss and will be able to remain within this experience for a very long time. In fact, this bliss will continue to be experienced unceasingly, even when you are no longer engaged in meditation. This practice of experiencing these stages of simultaneous great bliss and using such minds to meditate upon emptiness is of essential importance to the completion stage and you can beneficially spend your entire life within it.

It was mentioned earlier that sutra and secret mantra utilize different levels of mind to meditate upon objective emptiness. The most powerful of all such minds is that of simultaneous great bliss. It has far greater power to destroy the obscurations preventing liberation and omniscience than any other mind because such a blissful consciousness is completely free from all gross conceptual thoughts and dualistic appearances. Conceptions cannot disturb the mind of simultaneous great bliss because the winds supporting such conceptions have already been dissolved within the central channel and thus have ceased functioning. Because there is no longer any danger of interference from these gross conceptualizations, you will be able to meditate upon emptiness with great power and clarity. The subjective mind and the objective emptiness will mix indistinguishably as if you were pouring water into water.

In addition to being the most expedient method of eliminating the obstacles preventing liberation and omniscience, this meditation is also the quickest way to achieve the holy bodies of a buddha. The mind of simultaneous great bliss serves as the substantial cause of the holy truth body of a buddha while the wind upon which it is mounted is the substantial cause of a buddha's holy form body. In this way the meditation on simultaneous great bliss is also the best method of completing the two accumulations of wisdom and merit which are responsible for the achievement of the truth and form bodies respectively.

A meditator who is successful in these practices need not engage in any other spiritual activity. For those who are fortunate enough to be proficient in such methods, all their daily actions—whether walking, eating or whatever—help complete the collections of merit and wisdom. Secret mantra is called the quick path because the meditation on simultaneous great bliss and emptiness cuts the two obscurations and completes the two collections. Thus one practice achieves all results. However, some people have a completely mistaken view of secret mantra. Without having any experience of great bliss and emptiness they nevertheless claim, 'I am a secret mantra yogi' and use this as an excuse to drink alcohol, smoke, take drugs, dispute, engage in sexual misconduct and so forth. But engaging in harmful conduct should not be considered the same as following the path of secret mantra. After all, such actions can be performed by anyone. Those who have the pure wish to become true yogis of secret mantra should instead put a great deal of effort into mastering the meditation just described and should do so with an impeccable bodhicitta motivation.

When the white drop melts and eventually reaches the tip of the sex organ, the simultaneous joy of the serial order is experienced and this continues for as long as the white drop remains there. Then, through the force of the dissolved winds, the flow of the white drop is reversed and as this drop ascends the central channel the four joys of the reverse order are experienced. As stated, all five are stages of simultaneous great bliss and each stage is more intense than the one preceding it. If these experiences are analyzed in more detail it will be possible to differentiate sixteen joys of the serial order and another sixteen of the reverse. For example, when the white drop descends one quarter of the way between the crown and throat channel-wheels the first division of the first joy is experienced. Each stage of joy is similarly divided into four divisions of increasing intensity, thereby accounting for a total of thirty-two stages of blissful experience in all.

While abiding in the simultaneous joy of the reverse order your primary mind will become completely transformed into the nature of simultaneous great bliss. Such a consciousness is both a primary mind and a subtle one. According to sutra, bliss can only be a mental factor and not a primary mind but this is not true in terms of secret mantra. Here there is a mind of simultaneous great bliss which is also a primary mind.

The substantial cause of the illusory body is the very subtle wind mounted by the very subtle mind of clear light meditating upon emptiness. When the meditator arises from the session in which the isolated mind of ultimate example clear light is achieved, he or she will take a body that is not the same as his or her previous physical body. Rather, it will be the same in appearance as the body of the personal deity of the generation stage, but white in colour. Such a form, however, can only be perceived by someone who has already attained the illusory body. In this respect, then, this illusory body is similar to a dream body and the common cause for both is the very subtle wind. In fact, as stated in the *Guhyasamaja Tantra*, the dream body is considered the best example to explain the illusory body and can be taken as proof of its potential existence.

There are two times at which it is possible to attain the isolated mind of ultimate example clear light: (1) prior to the clear light of death and (2) at the time of the clear light of death. If it is attained *prior* to death then it is definite that the meditator will achieve enlightenment while still possessing his or her gross physical form. If it is attained *at* death, then the clear light of death itself will transform into the isolated mind of ultimate example clear light and, instead of passing to the intermediate state, the meditator will achieve the illusory body. It is with this illusory body that enlightenment is achieved. When referring to this second case it is sometimes said that the meditator becomes a buddha in the intermediate state, or with an intermediate state body. In fact, however, such a meditator's body is not an actual intermediate state body at all; what he or she has achieved is the illusory body which is the deity's body.

In order to reach the isolated mind of ultimate example clear light, your power of meditation on the channels, winds and drops must have been completed. Furthermore in order to reach the isolated mind of ultimate example clear light *before* the clear light of death, it is necessary to accept a qualified action seal. The highly-realized lama Je Tsong-khapa did not accept such an action seal because he was concerned for the welfare of his monk and nun followers. Although he himself was at the stage where he could have meditated with an action seal consort without creating the slightest negativity, even though he was a monk, he did not do so. Why not? He wished to protect those impatient disciples of the future who, thinking they could follow his example without being fully qualified, would have been tempted to take a consort and thus would have fallen to migrations of deep suffering.

Je Tsong-khapa was widely praised during his lifetime and afterwards by many great yogis for his lucid and unique exposition of secret mantra practices. He was especially famous for his explanations of the means for attaining the illusory body. He demonstrated the way of achieving the four empties of the isolated mind through the force of the vajra recitation of the *Guhyasamaja Tantra* and, when he was about to leave his gross physical body, he achieved the isolated mind of ultimate example clear light by mixing the son and mother clear lights. On the twenty-fifth day of the tenth Tibetan month he achieved this isolated mind and when he arose from that meditation he attained the illusory body with which he reached enlightenment. In actuality, however, Je Tsong-khapa was already the fully enlightened Buddha Manjushri. But in order to benefit others Manjushri appears in many forms: enlightened and ordinary, ordained and lay. In this case he appeared as a revered teacher who, in his life and works, demonstrated the pure sutra and secret mantra paths to full enlightenment and gave his fortunate disciples an excellent example to emulate. The actions of enlightened beings such as Manjushri are beyond the scope of the minds of ordinary beings.

In general there are four joys of the generation stage and four of the completion stage. To attain the former it is not absolutely necessary to bring the winds into the central channel; these four joys are mainly attained through the force of meditative concentration. As for the latter, they result from the melting and flowing of the white drop within the central channel. You should rehearse for this experience by practising the four joys of the generation stage as described in the tantras of Guhyasamaja, Heruka, Vajrayogini and so forth and by following the instructions of a fully-qualified tantric master.

The four joys of the completion stage are practised in conjunction with the inner fire meditation and other methods such as the vajra recitation and so forth. First you should perform the eight rounds of inner fire meditation as described earlier. The heat generated from this will melt the white drop at the crown which will flow down the central channel from the crown to the throat, from the throat to the heart, from the heart to the navel and from the navel to the tip of the sex organ. This will bring with it the experience of simultaneous joy and you should maintain this experience while meditating upon emptiness. Then you should generate the four joys of the reverse order—all of which are stages of simultaneous great bliss—and thereby continue meditating upon emptiness with a supremely blissful mind. This concludes the explanation of the four joys.

4 The Nine Mixings and the Two Seals

The practice of the nine mixings (28)

The nine mixings are the main methods for taking ordinary death, the intermediate state and rebirth as the paths to the truth, enjoyment and emanation bodies of a fully enlightened buddha. These nine are extensively explained in the texts of *Guhyasamaja Tantra* and both Nagarjuna and his disciple Aryadeva wrote explicit commentaries on this practice. These teachings were brought from India to Tibet where they have been practised down to the present day.

The nine mixings make up one of the essential practices of completion stage meditation and it is not possible to attain buddhahood within one short lifetime without them. Both Marpa and Milarepa had special praise for this practice and the great meditator Kedrub Rinpoche (1385-1438) said that even if one does not gain the complete experience of these nine mixings, a great stock of merit can be accumulated merely through acquiring an intellectual understanding of them. In short, all qualified meditators of the completion stage of secret mantra rely upon the practice of the nine mixings. The instructions which follow have been extracted from Vajradhara's teachings contained in the *Guhyasamaja Tantra* from where they were grafted onto other highest yoga tantra practices.

The nine mixings are explained in three major divisions:

The mixings during waking (29)
This is also divided into three parts:

The mixing with the truth body during waking (30)

The first of the nine mixings is the mixing with the truth body during waking. As has already been explained, through the force of inner fire meditation, the winds are made to enter, abide and dissolve into the central channel. As a result the meditator experiences the eight signs from the mirage-like appearance to the clear light. This clear light is to be transformed into the path by meditating upon emptiness. It is in this way that the clear light is mixed with the truth body and meditating in this fashion is called 'mixing with the truth body during waking'. It should be noted however, that at this time there is no actual truth body with which the clear light can be mixed. The meditator merely imagines that this clear light is the actual truth body and then proceeds with the practices. According to secret mantra, there are three types of truth body: (1) the basic truth body, (2) the path truth body and (3) the fruit or resultant truth body. Despite their titles, the first two are not the actual truth body. However, on the foundation of the basic truth body and through the practices of the path truth body the state of enlightenment is eventually attained. When this happens the meditator achieves the resultant truth body, that is the actual truth body of a buddha.

The practice of the mixing with the truth body during waking can be explained as follows. As before, the initial object of meditation is the *short a* in the centre of the navel channel-wheel. You should concentrate on this object until you experience the eight signs mentioned before. Throughout the entire progression of the eight signs it is very important not to forget emptiness, for if you do not remember emptiness with the gross mind it will be impossible to realize it with the subtle mind. Therefore, when the mirage-like appearance is experienced, remember that this appearance does not naturally exist from its own side; think that it is merely an appearance to your perceiving consciousness. Then employ the same type of memory throughout the next three signs: those of smoke, fireflies and the candle flame. After all of these have been experienced, your gross memory or mindfulness will disappear. During the next appearance, which is the first of the four empties—the mind of white appearance—only your subtle memory will be functioning.

During the mind of white appearance the only perception will be of an empty sky pervaded by the bright white light of an autumn full moon. Remember that the emptiness of this first empty is the emptiness of inherent existence. Because the mind at this point is a subtle mind, it will be difficult initially to establish the emptiness of inherent existence through the force of logical reasoning. However, as you become more familiar with the experience of the subtle mind, you will be able to use logical reasoning to establish such an emptiness even during the mind of white appearance.

From the mind of white appearance you then move to the mind of red increase, perceived somewhat like the empty sky pervaded by the red light of the sun. As before you should maintain your memory of emptiness; you should meditate that the emptiness of this second empty is the emptiness of inherent existence. Then when the mind of black near-attainment arises, which is perceived as an empty sky pervaded by blackness, you should maintain your memory of emptiness until the profound swoon of this subtle mind is experienced. During this swoon you will be forced to lose the memory of emptiness temporarily, because at this time there is no conscious activity whatsoever.

After the cessation of the mind of black near-attainment, the very subtle mind of clear light, the subtlest of all minds, will arise. This very subtle mind will perceive an appearance like that of an empty autumn sky at dawn pervaded by a clear and radiant light. With this very subtle mind of clear light you should meditate on the emptiness of this fourth empty as being the emptiness of inherent existence. The ability to remember emptiness at such a time depends upon having been able to remember emptiness during the preceding empties, with the momentary exception of the profound swoon of the black appearance. Remembering emptiness during the appearance of the subtle minds depends on having remembered emptiness with the gross mind prior to its dissolution. Thus it is important not to forget emptiness right from the very beginning of the mirage-like appearance.

When the very subtle mind of clear light meditates upon emptiness and holds this union of clear light and emptiness to be similar in aspect to the truth body, you will be practising the first of the three mixings. It is not sufficient to do this one or two times only; it is necessary to practise in this way continuously until realization is achieved. On the basis of mixing with the truth body during waking you should develop the divine pride of having the actual truth body of a buddha and in this way make your realization of the truth body absolutely indestructible.

As indicated earlier, during the generation stage of secret mantra meditation you take death as the path of the truth body. The purpose of this is to prepare for and facilitate the mixing with the truth body that you practise during the completion stage. Mixing with the truth body during waking facilitates the mixing with the truth body during sleep, which in turn facilitates the mixing with the truth body during death. When your very subtle mind of clear light meditates upon emptiness, you have reached the first realization of mahamudra according to secret mantra.

The mixing with the enjoyment body during waking (31)

This is the second of the nine mixings. Through generating

the divine pride of having the truth body, which is free of deceptive dualistic appearances, you have made your realization of the truth body indestructible. This clear light mind has a similar aspect to the clear light mind of death. As explained, after the experience of the clear light of death, ordinary beings take an intermediate state body. The accomplished meditator however, takes the body of his or her personal deity in place of such an ordinary intermediate state body. Therefore, when you are practising the second of the nine mixings you should meditate that you arise from the clear light state of emptiness, or the truth body, in the form of your personal deity. If your personal deity is Heruka, then with divine pride think that you have arisen in his form. However, instead of being blue in colour, your holy body is white and you embrace a white Vajravarahi. You should meditate that the very subtle wind mounted by the mind of clear light arises in the form of Heruka's holy body and that the very subtle mind of clear light itself is Heruka's holy mind. With divine pride meditate that now you are the actual enjoyment body of the buddha Heruka.

Practising in this way creates the cause for your future achievement of an actual illusory body in the form of your personal deity. Such an illusory body is not something that can be seen by everyone. Although it is an actual body, it is not perceivable by those who have not yet attained it. In general, this illusory body is called the enjoyment body of the path. As was the case with the truth body, according to secret mantra there are three types of enjoyment body: (1) the basic enjoyment body, (2) the path enjoyment body and (3) the fruit or resultant enjoyment body, the first two of which are enjoyment bodies in name only. After the attainment of the illusory body—the so-called enjoyment body of the path—the meditator practises continuously and eventually becomes a buddha, thereby attaining the resultant enjoyment body which is an actual body of a buddha.

In summary, when you arise from the appearance of clear light in the white form of your personal deity, you should focus upon that white form and develop the divine pride that thinks, 'Now I am the actual enjoyment body.' This is the practice of mixing with the enjoyment body during waking. Such a practice facilitates mixing with the enjoyment body during sleep, which in turn facilitates the mixing with the enjoyment body during death. All of these are preceded by the generation stage practice in which you take the intermediate state to the path of the enjoyment body and thereby rehearse for and facilitate the mixings with the enjoyment body performed during completion stage meditation.

The mixing with the emanation body during waking (32)

Now comes the practice of the third of the nine mixings. At this point you are still in the form of the white enjoyment body of your personal deity. You should understand that this body and your normal physical body are totally different. Then think like this: 'If I remain in this state, ordinary beings will not be able to perceive me and I shall therefore be unable to help them pass beyond suffering and attain buddhahood.' On the basis of this thought and your bodhicitta motivation, you should then make a strong determination to take an emanation body for the benefit of others. Such an emanation body can be perceived by ordinary beings and therefore allows you to be of maximum benefit to others.

Prior to practising the mixings during waking, you had generated yourself in the aspect of your personal deity. Such a being is called the commitment being. For example, if your personal deity is Heruka, the commitment being is yourself in the form of Heruka, blue in colour with one face and two hands. Such a commitment being body is present throughout completion stage meditation, but it ceases to be an object of meditation while you are practising the mixings with the truth and enjoyment bodies. This is similar to the way in which the appearance of your ordinary body ceases when you fall asleep and dream, for although your physical body does remain you are no longer aware of it.

Now, after the mixing with the truth body, you have arisen

as the illusory body in the form of white Heruka. This white Heruka differs from the blue commitment being body in much the same way that a dream body differs from a gross physical body. While you practise the mixing with the enjoyment body, you develop the strong divine pride of being the actual enjoyment body of Heruka. This white Heruka becomes what is known as the wisdom being. When, as a result of your strong bodhicitta motivation, you determine to arise in the form of an emanation body for the benefit of others, meditate that this white Heruka enters the commitment being's body through the crown of its head. This is similar to the way in which upon waking from a dream, your dream body re-enters into your gross physical body. At this point in your meditation white Heruka remains in the heart of the emanation body—the blue Heruka—as a wisdom being. Focussing on the body of blue Heruka, you should develop the divine pride of being the actual emanation body. This practice is known as mixing with the emanation body during waking and thus concludes the explanation of the first third of the nine mixings.

The mixings during sleep (33)

As was the case with the mixings during waking, this section is divided into three parts:

34 The mixing with the truth body during sleep
35 The mixing with the enjoyment body during sleep
36 The mixing with the emanation body during sleep

The mixing with the truth body during sleep (34)

When ordinary beings fall asleep they experience the clear light of sleep. The meditator of secret mantra endeavours to mix this clear light of sleep with the truth body. But this can only be accomplished by those who have previously gained experience in the four empties by practising the mixings during waking as described above. Therefore, such meditation can only be successful if you are able to cause your winds to enter, abide and dissolve within the central channel.

When you are going to practise the mixings during sleep, you should meditate upon the inner fire immediately before falling asleep. At this time you need not be sitting up in the normal meditation posture; you can practise inner fire while lying in your normal sleeping position. If possible, however, it is good to sleep in the so-called 'lion posture'. Lie down on your right side and rest your right cheek on the palm of your right hand. Your legs should be straight with your left resting upon your right and your left arm outstretched on top. This posture, in which Shakyamuni Buddha passed away, is an excellent one to assume whenever you are going to sleep.

As in the normal inner fire practice, the object of meditation is the *short a* in the vacuole within the centre of the navel channel-wheel. If you are familiar with and proficient in causing the winds to enter, abide and dissolve within the central channel during waking, you should be able to do the same during sleep without much difficulty. Therefore, practise the inner fire meditation until you perceive the mirage-like appearance of sleep. While falling asleep you must be able to identify each appearance as it arises through the force of mindfulness. You must also remember the emptiness of inherent existence from the very beginning of the mirage-like appearance up to and including the fourth empty, which is clear light itself. Think that these eight signs are mere appearances perceived by your primary mind and that they are empty, lacking true, inherent self-existence. When, during the eighth sign, your very subtle mind of clear light meditates upon emptiness, your experience of emptiness will become extremely powerful. This is because the very subtle mind can mingle with its object like water being poured into water. When you reach this point in your practice, you should meditate that the nonduality of your mind and emptiness has become absolutely indestructible. This is the practice of mixing with the truth body during sleep.

There are two profound methods, to be practised consecutively, by which this meditation is accomplished: (1) causing the winds to enter, abide and dissolve within the central channel during waking and thereby being able to do the same during sleep and (2) not allowing the power of memory to decline during sleep. The first method has already been discussed; what follows is an explanation of the second.

In general, when you fall asleep you completely lose the power of memory or mindfulness. Therefore, you do not recognize the eight signs of sleep as they occur. Moreover, if the power of your mindfulness does *not* decline, you find it impossible to fall asleep at all. Therefore, you must be very skilful in practising the mixings with the truth body during sleep; you must be able to fall asleep yet still maintain the power of memory. The way to practise, then, is to allow your memory to decline very slightly, just enough to make sleep possible but not to the extent that you are unable to recognize even the first of the eight signs of sleep. In general, when most beings are asleep and when they are dreaming they are not conscious of the fact that they are dreaming. This is the result of their memory having declined completely. The accomplished meditator, on the other hand, is able to identify the eight signs as being the eight signs of sleep and also knows when he or she has entered the dream state.

When you lie down to sleep, therefore, you should practise the meditation on inner fire with the principal object of meditation being the *short a* within the centre of the navel channel-wheel. While you are doing this, with a portion of your mind you should determine to maintain your memory and recognize the eight signs as they appear and also to know them as being empty of inherent existence. If you practise continuously, the forces of concentration and determination will bring you success in this practice. A strong sense of determination is very important. When you determine from the beginning to recognize the eight signs of sleep, such a strong decision will enable you to accomplish your purpose. Success in this will be even easier if while practising the mixings during waking you remember that the same eight signs will occur when you fall asleep. For example, when the mirage-like appearance arises during your waking practice, you should remind yourself that this sign will also arise when you are asleep.

Although ordinary beings do perceive the clear light while dying and while falling asleep, they are unable to recognize this experience as being the clear light. The accomplished meditator, however, does have such a recognition and uses it as the quickest vehicle to spiritual awakening. He or she is able to perceive the clear light during the time of sleep even more vividly than the clear light perceived when mixing with the truth body during waking. Therefore, mixing with the truth body during sleep can be an even more powerful meditation than that done during waking.

When the great bodhisattva Shantideva (c.685 A.D.) was staying at the great monastic university of Nalanda, the other monks felt that he did only three things: eat, defecate and sleep—and mostly the latter! Observing his behaviour, they thought that Shantideva was extremely lazy; in reality, however, he was engaged in very advanced secret mantra practices of the three mixings during sleep. Therefore, if one is truly a skilled meditator, sleep itself can become a powerful spiritual practice.

When mixing with the truth body during sleep, you should try to integrate the experience of the four empties gained during waking meditation with the four empties experienced while falling asleep. It is through the integration of these two that your meditation will become very powerful. But to practise the mixings during sleep well, your sleep should be long, deep and undisturbed. If you are interrupted during your sleeping meditation, this will interfere with your ability to meditate on the clear light. For example, if after experiencing the first two signs of sleep you are awakened or disturbed by something, this will interfere with your perception of the remaining signs and thus your practice of mixing with the truth body during sleep will be interrupted. As Aryadeva asked in his *Lamp of Condensed Deeds*, 'What is the cause of a long deep sleep?' Aryadeva's own answer states that it is by causing the winds to gather forcefully at the heart that you will experience a long and deep sleep. The more forcefully these winds gather within the heart, the longer and deeper the sleep will be.

Because a long deep sleep is the best type for the practice of the mixings, you should try to have the winds gather within your heart by means of the following visualization. While falling asleep focus your mind upon the indestructible drop within the centre of your heart channel-wheel. Concentrate your mind upon this drop and allow yourself to fall asleep. Or, if you prefer, you can visualize *any* letter at your heart. For instance, the practitioner of inner fire meditation can use the *short a*. In the beginning, concentrate on this *short a* of inner fire as it resides within the navel channel-wheel. Then, immediately before falling asleep, move the letter up through the central channel until it reaches the vacuole of the heart channel-wheel where the indestructible drop resides. Then, as you fall asleep, visualize this *short a* in your heart.

There is another method that is effective in producing a long and deep sleep and it is especially helpful if you want to fall asleep quickly. First visualize that the indestructible drop in the centre of your heart is in the form of a radiant white drop. This drop then descends the central channel and finally comes to rest at the tip of the sex organ where it transforms into a black drop. Then fall asleep while concentrating upon this black drop. As it is much easier to perceive the eight signs during a long and deep sleep, you should use whichever method you find most useful for attaining this goal. Even if you are not ready to begin the actual practice of the mixings during sleep, it is important to start your training now so that the seeds of this practice will be planted and cultivated within your mind. This is true for all nine of the mixings.

To summarize, then, when you are qualified to practise the mixings during sleep, the longer you sleep the better.

You need not be practising the methods of secret mantra to

gain the conscious recognition of your sleep as being sleep and of your dreams as being dreams. Such a recognition can be achieved merely through the forces of determination and concentration. While you are in the waking state you should make the strong and constant determination to recognize your sleep as sleep and to recognize your dreams as dreams when they arise. Then, by virtue of firm concentration, you will be able to attain these two conscious recognitions. When you are actually practising secret mantra, these two recognitions are gained by causing the winds to enter, abide and dissolve within the central channel as well as by the force of concentration. If you have previously become accustomed to the experience of the four empties by having practised the mixings during waking, it will not be difficult to recognize these four empties when you are asleep.

In conclusion, when you perceive the clear light of sleep you should use that mind to meditate upon emptiness. If you are able to do this practice, you will be mixing the son and mother clear lights of sleep and, as a result, you will be able to mix the son and mother clear lights of death as well. While you are awake the only clear light that can be experienced is the son clear light; therefore, the only time you can mix the son and mother clear lights prior to your actual death is while you are asleep. If you are successful in this, then even your sleep will become a powerful and beneficial meditation. This ends the discussion of the practice of mixing with the truth body during sleep.

The mixing with the enjoyment body during sleep (35)
This practice, the fifth of the nine mixings, is carried out while you are dreaming. It is only while you are experiencing the dream state that you have the opportunity to practise this particular mixing.

In general, there are two types of sleep, that without dreams and that with dreams. The sleep experienced during the evolution of the eight signs is sleep without dreams. Dreams will arise once the clear light of sleep ceases. This is very similar to the manner in which the intermediate state arises immediately following the cessation of the clear light of death.

Sleep without dreams is also of two types: light sleep and deep sleep. Light sleep is experienced up until the third empty, that is the mind of black near-attainment. From the mirage-like appearance to the mind of red increase, one's sleep is classified as being light though the sleep gets progressively deeper with the appearance of each successive sign. The deepest sleep of all is experienced during the mind of black near-attainment. It is at this time that all memory is strongly and temporarily lost.

From the beginning of the mirage-like appearance the secret mantra practitioner holds onto emptiness as the object of meditation, but the ability to hold this object ceases for a while during the experience of the mind of black near-attainment. When the fourth empty, or all empty—which is the clear light itself—gradually dawns, you regain a very subtle memory. It is through this force of very subtle memory that you will be able to mix the son and the mother clear lights of sleep. This will enable you to transform the clear light of sleep into the actual truth body of the path or into a truth body of the path that is similar to it. The actual truth body of the path is the example and meaning clear light.

You will not experience any dreams until the clear light of sleep ceases. After mixing with the truth body during sleep, when the clear light of sleep has been transformed into the path truth body, the secret mantra meditator practises the mixing with the enjoyment body during sleep. This is done by transforming the ordinary dream state into the enjoyment body of the path. While still in the form of the truth body, the meditator determines to attain the enjoyment body for the sake of others. After this strong determination is set the dream state will arise. When it does the accomplished meditator will be able to recognize it for what it is and will thereby be able to transform his or her dream body into the enjoyment body of the path. The meditator then attempts to arise in the form of his or her personal deity, which is white in colour, has one face and two hands and embraces a white wisdom consort. In this way the meditator is able to transform the ordinary dream state into the actual enjoyment body of the path or into an enjoyment body of the path which is similar to it.

The actual enjoyment body of the path arises from the isolated mind of ultimate example clear light. Such a mind has two parts: the mind itself and its mounted wind. The mind is the very subtle mind of clear light realizing emptiness. It is from this mind and its mounted wind that the illusory body develops. As indicated earlier, the illusory body is altogether different from the gross physical body. When you attain the illusory body, its shape is the same as that of your personal diety. Such an illusory body is an actual body but is only perceived by someone who has achieved it. This is similar to the way in which a dream body is only perceived by the dreamer. When the illusory body is attained, your subtle form will transform into the aspect of your personal deity. This illusory body is the actual enjoyment body of the path. When mixing with the enjoyment body during sleep, you transform the dream body into either the actual enjoyment body of the path or into a similar enjoyment body.

Dream sleep is also a form of light sleep. To be able to use such sleep in your practice, your dreams should be very long and clear and you should have a strongly developed power of memory so that you can recognize your dreams for what they are and thereby be able to transform the dream body into the enjoyment body of the path. As long as your dream body continues you should try to maintain this transformation as well as the divine pride of actually possessing the resultant enjoyment body of a buddha. When the secret mantra meditator realizes that the dream will soon end, he or she prepares to practise the sixth of the nine mixings: the mixing with the emanation body during sleep.

The mixing with the emanation body during sleep (36)

The sixth mixing can be explained by using the practice of Heruka as an example. During the dream state you are in the white form of the enjoyment body of Heruka. Then you should think that if you were to remain in that form ordinary beings would not be able to see you, because only arya bodhisattvas and buddhas are able to perceive the enjoyment body of a buddha. Therefore, you should make the strong determination to arise in the form of an emanation body that even ordinary beings can see and benefit from.

After generating the strong bodhicitta motivation, you will awaken from the sleep of the dream state. The way in which this should be done is very important. Practising the mixings during sleep is very similar to practising the mixings during waking. Before you went to sleep, you were visualizing yourself as the Heruka commitment being, blue in colour, with one face and two hands and embracing his consort. While practising the mixings with the truth and enjoyment bodies during sleep, you lose this appearance of the commitment being. When you enter the dream state, you arise from the clear light of sleep in the form of white Heruka, thereby transforming the dream body into the enjoyment body. This white Heruka is destined to become the wisdom being when you practise the mixing with the emanation body during sleep. Thus the commitment being's body and the enjoyment body are different entities in the same way that the gross physical body is different from the dream body. When you practise the mixing with the emanation body during sleep, you should cause the enjoyment body to enter the commitment being's body in the same way that the dream body enters the gross physical body when you awaken from the dream state. When the white Heruka enters the blue Heruka it becomes the wisdom being and remains in the heart of the blue Heruka. At this time you have awakened and you should do so with the thought, 'I am the real resultant emanation body; I am Heruka.'

In summary, then, you arise from the dream state in the form of blue Heruka and generate the strong divine pride of possessing the emanation body of a buddha. Even though this divine pride is generated while awake, this practice is called 'the mixing with the emanation body during sleep'. The reason is that this process of mixing began with the strong determination generated while still in the sleep of the dream state.

While practising the three mixings of sleep, the sleep and dream times are said to belong to the equipoise meditation session and the awakening in the form of the emanation body is classified as belonging to the post meditation, or subsequent realization, session. During the subsequent realization session an accomplished meditator will practise three yogas no matter what appears to his or her sense perceptions. Namely, (1) the meditator will contemplate all appearances as being empty of inherent existence; (2) he or she will regard all these emptinesses as being in the nature of bliss and (3) he or she will perceive this bliss as being in the form of the personal deity's body. Such an accomplished meditator performs all the activities of the subsequent realization session without ever being separated from the practice of these three yogas. This section is concluded with the five questions and answers concerning the mixings during sleep that Aryadeva included in his *Lamp of Condensed Deeds.*

(1) *What is the cause of sleep in general and of a long and deep sleep in particular?* Sleep occurs when the five gross winds— the mounts of the five sense conciousness—gather naturally within the heart. Until these winds gather there, it will be impossible to fall asleep. In fact, if you are having trouble in getting to sleep it is because these winds are not gathering at the heart for one reason or another. Sometimes these winds gather naturally even when we do not wish them to; for example, during teachings or in the middle of a meditation session you might find yourself falling asleep uncontrollably. Some of the causes for this unwished for gathering of the winds at the heart are mental sinking, dullness, physical tiredness, overeating, lack of sleep the previous night and so forth.

As for the cause of a long and deep sleep, this occurs when the winds not only gather naturally at the heart but do so forcefully. It should be noted that in addition to the natural process of gathering, the winds of the five sense conscious-

nesses can also collect at the heart through the force of meditation as well as at the time of death. In neither of these two
cases does sleep occur because the gathering of the winds does
not happen naturally.

(2) *What is the cause of dreams in general and of long and clear
dreams in particular?* As stated above, as long as the winds
remain in the heart one generally experiences a state of deep
sleep. When these winds leave the heart and gather in the
throat, you move from the state of deep sleep to the lighter
state of dream sleep. In other words, when the drop in the
throat channel-wheel and the winds meet the dream state will
arise. Furthermore, the cause of long and clear dreams is that
the winds not only gather within the throat but that they do so
forcefully. As long as the winds are collected in the throat you
will be in the dream state and the longer and more forcefully
they gather there the longer and more clear your dreams will
be.

(3) *What causes the dream body to enter the gross body when
you awaken from the dream state?* Even when your dream body
travels to a far distant dream place, when you wake up this
dream body enters your gross body immediately. This happens because the dream body has left the gross body only temporarily and the relationship that exists between the two of
them has not yet come to an end. As long as their karmic link
is not severed, the dream body will always return to the gross
body. This is analogous to the situation in which the father of
a family makes a pilgrimage to India. He only leaves his family
temporarily and when the pilgrimage is completed he will
return to them. He does so because of the relationship he has
with his family. However, if for some reason that relationship
or connection comes to an end the father will be unable to
return as he had originally planned. Returning to the dream
situation, the place the dream body travels to is not an actual
place, it is a dream place.

(4) *If the dream body and the gross body are different, why do
the experiences of the dream body ripen upon the gross body?* A
person might wake up from a terrifying nightmare to discover

that his or her heart is pounding and palms are perspiring. Furthermore, a man may merely dream of having sexual intercourse yet actually lose semen. The reason that these things can happen is that the mind of the dreaming person and the mind of the waking person belong to the same continuum. Only one person exists in relation to this continuum and therefore the experiences of his or her dreaming mind can ripen upon the waking mind. It should be noted that the reverse can also happen. For example some people have the experience of being rained upon while sleeping with the result that they dream that they are swimming or drowning.

(5) *What is the cause of waking from sleep?* When the winds leave the throat and gather at the brow, you wake up from the dream state. In fact, if you wish to arise quickly from sleep with an alert and clear mind, you should visualize a white drop in the forehead channel-wheel and concentrate on it before falling asleep. As stated before, wherever the mind focusses there will its mounted wind gather. And it is the gathering of the winds into the brow that causes the awakening from sleep.

The mixings during death (37)

There is only one opportunity in each life to practise the mixings during death. Thus it is very important that you train for this during your lifetime. This is done by practising the mixings during sleep and success in this depends upon being proficient in practising the mixings during waking. The easiest of these interrelated sets of practices are the mixings during waking because they offer more opportunity to make use of your gross memory.

As stated, successful practice of the mixings during death depends upon proficiency in the mixings during sleep. If you are unable to practise the mixings with the truth, enjoyment and emanation bodies during sleep, you will be unable to mix with them during death. On the other hand, if you are able to do the practices during sleep you will also be able to do them during death because, generally speaking, the process of falling asleep and the process of dying are very similar. In both cases the winds gather at the heart.

At the time of death you will experience the eight signs from the mirage-like appearance to the clear light of death. An accomplished meditator combines the eight signs of dying with the eight signs that occur when the winds dissolve into the central channel through the force of completion stage meditation. It is in this way that the meditator transforms the eight signs of dying into the spiritual path. Of course, here we are talking about the meditator who has practised secret mantra meditation and has not attained enlightenment during his or her lifetime. As was stated earlier, if someone has already attained enlightenment during his or her lifetime, there will be no need to practise the three mixings during death because ordinary death has already been overcome. Yet life is very short and death may come even to a great meditator before final enlightenment is reached; if this happens then it is necessary to practise the mixings during death.

If you are unable to practise these mixings during death, then you will have to take an ordinary samsaric rebirth without any choice. This brings with it the danger that all the spiritual knowledge you have gained in this lifetime will be forgotten. This would be a great shame. Dying without conscious control brings with it a loss of everything you tried so hard to learn in this life; only the imprints of this knowledge will remain. Even if you have the fortune to be reborn a human being in your future life, you have to begin all over again going through the same problems of gathering knowledge that you encountered before. On the other hand, if you die with control you will be able to carry the practice of this life with you into the next life. Only your physical body will have changed; the knowledge you have gathered will remain intact.

It is very important to die with a happy and positive mind. Even though you might practise very hard in this life, if you die with an angry or negative mind you will fall to one of the three states of unfortunate migration. Therefore, while you are dying you should be very mindful of your mental activity and check to see if it is positive and virtuous or not. The true test of an accomplished meditator is whether he or she can maintain the practice of dharma during the evolution of the death process.

When you practise the mixings during waking you should remember that the purpose is to be able to practise them during sleep. Likewise, when practising during sleep you should remember that the purpose is to be able to practise them during death. As for the practices during death itself, these have three major purposes: (1) to protect you from fear throughout the death process, (2) to give you the power to choose the circumstances of your future rebirth and (3) to enable you to carry this life's practice into the future life. These three reasons alone are sufficient to demonstrate how precious the vajrayana doctrine is. Furthermore, by practising the vajrayana in a perfect and pure manner, you will certainly be able to reach enlightenment in your future life if you are unable to do so during this one.

As with the mixings practised during waking and sleep, the mixings during death are divided into three parts:

38 The mixing with the truth body during death
39 The mixing with the enjoyment body during death
40 The mixing with the emanation body during death

The mixing with the truth body during death (38)

You should begin this practice as soon as you are certain that you are dying. Select an object of meditation that will cause your winds to enter, abide and dissolve within the central channel. If during your lifetime your main practice was inner fire, you should use that as your object of meditation now and continue practising it until you die. If you practise the inner fire during the death process, the eight signs will appear very clearly.

When these eight signs do appear you should meditate upon their lack of inherent existence. Such a meditation should be done from the very beginning from the mirage-like appearance and continue throughout all eight signs. When you reach the clear light of death, you should not lose the power of your memory but rather, through the force of that memory, you should meditate upon emptiness with that very subtle mind of clear light. As stated before, ordinary beings lose the power of their memory during the process of dying and therefore are unable to recognize the clear light even when it arises. The accomplished meditator is able to retain his or her memory because of previous intensive training during that lifetime in the mixings of waking and sleep. Therefore such a meditator is not only able to recognize such a clear light but is also able to meditate upon emptiness with that very subtle mind. It is in this way that the ordinary clear light of death is transformed into the truth body of the path.

During the mind of clear light you should generate the divine pride of having actually obtained the resultant truth body. This will make the seventh mixing indestructible.

The mixing with the enjoyment body during death (39)

When meditating upon the truth body of the path, you concentrate upon emptiness with the mind of clear light. This is your main practice, but with a slight portion of your mind you should determine that when the time of the intermediate state arrives you will arise in the form of the enjoyment body. If you have gained proficiency in recognizing sleep as sleep and dreams as dreams, you will also be able to recognize the intermediate state as being what it is.

Through the force of the previous determination, the accomplished meditator is able to prevent the appearance of the ordinary intermediate state from arising and in its place can take the form of the personal meditational deity. Thus, if Heruka is your personal deity, you should transform the intermediate state body into Heruka's holy body, white in colour with one face and two hands and embracing wisdom consort.

You should now meditate with divine pride that you have attained the resultant enjoyment body of a buddha.

The person who can meditate in the manner described has carried the practice of the previous life into the intermediate state. This intermediate state being has control in choosing the circumstances of the next rebirth and can appear wherever he or she wishes, for example in Vajrayogini's pure land or in another buddha field. Such a practitioner has succeeded in mixing with the enjoyment body during death.

It is important to remember the specific meanings of the terms employed here. The enjoyment body that has been achieved here is the enjoyment body of the path, not the actual resultant enjoyment body of a buddha. As stated, the ordinary intermediate state is called the basic enjoyment body according to the terminology of secret mantra. Through the force of the isolated mind of ultimate example clear light, the accomplished meditator will attain the illusory body—or, to use its synonym, the enjoyment body of the path—in place of the ordinary intermediate state body. The intermediate state body and the illusory body both arise from the same substance: the very subtle wind; when the actual resultant body of a buddha is obtained, this will also be through the force of the very subtle wind. It should be remembered that although the basic and path enjoyment bodies have the name enjoyment body, they are not the actual enjoyment body, i.e. the resultant enjoyment body, of a buddha.

To summarize, when you mix with the enjoyment body during death you arise from the clear light in the white form of your personal deity. Thus, depending upon your previous practices, you arise as either white Heruka, white Vajrayogini and so forth. The white colour is symbolic of the illusory body because the substance of this illusory body—the very subtle wind—is also white. Then, with divine pride you meditate that you have attained the resultant enjoyment body of a buddha and this is the entire practice of mixing with the enjoyment body during death.

The mixing with the emanation body during death (40)

At this point the meditator is ready to practise the ninth and last of the nine mixings: mixing with the emanation body during death. This practice begins while the meditator is still in the process of mixing with the enjoyment body. While still holding the divine pride of being the resultant enjoyment body, the meditator determines to arise in the aspect of the emanation body for the sake of all beings. Therefore you should think, 'If I remain in the form of the enjoyment body forever, ordinary beings will not be able to perceive me and I will therefore be unable to help them. Furthermore, as I wish to complete my practice of secret mantra, I must take the emanation body.'

It is at this point that the accomplished meditator chooses his or her rebirth, which can be in a human realm or in one of the pure lands. For example, if you wish to be born as a human in conditions conducive to the continuing practice of secret mantra, you would think, 'As I still have not completed my practice of secret mantra, I should take rebirth in the human realm. Which country, therefore, would be most conducive to such practice?' Then, if you are an accomplished meditator, you will take rebirth in a country where secret mantra is taught by fully qualified masters. Unlike ordinary beings who from the intermediate state take rebirth in their mother's womb without conscious control or choice, the fully accomplished meditator can determine where and when he or she will be reborn.

A brief explanation of the process of conscious rebirth is as follows. If your personal deity is Heruka, you should regard your future mother as Vajravarahi and your future father as Heruka. Through the force of such visualization you block the ordinary appearances of your mother and father and carry the previous life's practice into the future life. From the intermediate state you regard your mother as being the commitment being and yourself as being the wisdom being. Then, when the red and white drops of your future father and mother mix, you enter that union of germ cells and develop the divine pride of having attained the resultant emanation body of a buddha. This emanation body is visualized as being blue in colour with one face and two hands and together with consort. (If your personal deity is Vajrayogini, this emanation body is seen as red in colour with one face and two hands.)

When the being thus conceived exits from the womb of the mother, ordinary beings will perceive him or her as an ordinary baby. This, however, is merely the external appearance; internally such a being has the unceasing divine pride of being the emanation body of a particular buddha although this will not be evident to others. One who has reached this level of practice is entitled to be called an emanation body or tulku. Simply remembering one's previous life is not sufficient reason to be called by such a title. In addition, the meditator must have consciously chosen the circumstances for his or her future rebirth.

In summary, an emanation body is someone who has died, passed through the intermediate state and taken rebirth, all with conscious control and without interrupting the continuity of his or her practice from one life to the next. Such is the practice of mixing with the emanation body during death. Again it should be noted that in this case the meditator has the divine pride of being the emanation body but does not in fact have the actual resultant emanation body of a buddha; this is only attained through the force of the resultant enjoyment body. The entire explanation of conscious rebirth given above pertains only to the meditator who has not achieved the isolated mind of ultimate example clear light during death. If he or she had attained such a clear light mind then, instead of achieving the intermediate state, he or she would have achieved the illusory body and through it would have reached enlightenment.

Of the two methods for developing the subjective simultaneous great bliss, the first—penetrating the vital points of your own body—has now been explained. As stated, by meditating upon your own channels, winds and drops you cause your winds to enter, abide and dissolve within your central channel; as a result the experience of simultaneous great bliss arises.

One might receive the impression that this practice is done only by males. That is a complete misconception. This meditation can be carried out equally by members of both sexes; the only prerequisite is that one should be appropriately empowered by a qualified master of secret mantra. Depending upon the empowerment and instructions you have received, during the generation stage you might visualize yourself in the form of a male or female deity regardless of your own sex. For example, men may visualize themselves as Heruka and women may visualize themselves as Vajrayogini or, if they prefer, men may visualize themselves as Vajrayogini and women may see themselves as Heruka. It makes no difference. If a monk's personal deity is Vajrayogini then he *must* generate himself in this female aspect just as all males with the same personal deity must do. The essential point of all these practices is to prevent ordinary appearances from arising. If a man finds it uncomfortable to see himself as Vajrayogini and if a woman experiences the same difficulty in seeing herself as Heruka, this is only because they have failed to overcome their ordinary appearances. Once this fault has been eliminated, it makes no difference whether you choose to see yourself as a male or female deity.

When considering the father/mother aspect of a highest yoga tantra deity—for example, when Heruka is depicted embracing Vajravarahi—it may appear that the two figures are two different entities in the same way that an ordinary husband and wife are two different people. However, although the external appearance is one of separateness, the internal significance of their divine embrace is the union of simultaneous great bliss and emptiness. Such bliss and emptiness are, respectively, the method and wisdom of Vajradhara—the secret mantra manifestation of the fully enlightened being—and are of the same essence. Unlike the minds of ordinary beings, the omniscient mind of a buddha can take on the appearance of form. Thus Vajradhara's mind, which is the mind of union of simultaneous great bliss and emptiness, can arise in the apparently dual form of the father and mother aspect of Heruka. In this case the method of great bliss appears in the aspect of Heruka himself, while the essentially identical wisdom of emptiness appears in the aspect of his consort Vajravarahi.

There are many effective methods for generating simultaneous great bliss. The vajra recitation explained in the *Guhyasamaja Tantra* is one such method while others are found in the tantras of Vajrabhairava and so forth. According to the system of mahamudra being explained here, simultaneous great bliss is developed mainly by relying on inner fire meditation through which the winds are caused to enter, abide and dissolve within the central channel. As each method explained in the highest yoga tantras is adequate in and of itself, there is no need to practise all of them in order to experience simultaneous great bliss. Once such bliss has been generated through any one of the methods, you can practise the nine mixings mentioned earlier in order to reach beyond the obscurations preventing both liberation and omniscience and thereby achieve full enlightenment. The attainment of this exalted state—after which you are effortlessly impelled by the altruistic bodhicitta motivation—is the purpose of generating simultaneous great bliss.

This concludes the explanation of generating simultaneous great bliss through penetrating the vital points of your own body.

Generating simultaneous bliss by penetrating the vital points of another's body (41)

This, the second method for developing simultaneous great bliss, is explained under two headings:

42 The practice with the action seal
43 The practice with the wisdom seal

The practice with the action seal (42)

The practice with the action seal (karma mudra) refers to the meditation with an actual consort. In order to practise with the action seal here at the completion stage you must already be familiar with causing your winds to enter, abide and dissolve within the central channel through the force of meditation. A person who cannot control the winds in this way through meditation cannot possibly do so through copulation. If someone wishes to practise by means of engaging in sexual activity with an action seal, he or she must generate simultaneous great bliss through control of the winds and then must meditate upon emptiness with this blissful mind. A lay practitioner who is currently unable to transform sexual activity into the path in this way should generate the strong aspiration and motivation to be able to do so in the future.

One's partner, the action seal itself, cannot be just anyone. This partner must have received the empowerments of secret mantra, must know the meaning of secret mantra, must be able to keep all the mantric pledges and, if possible, must have the experience of the completion stage—or at the very least a slight experience of the generation stage. If both the male and female meditators do have experience of the completion stage practices and are able to bring the winds into the central channel, then meditation with consort can be extremely beneficial. The winds enter the central channel more forcefully through meditation with consort than they do through meditation without a consort. For this reason the embrace of a consort is very helpful in bringing about a complete loosening of the channel knot at the heart channel-wheel. In fact, a person who has reached the isolated mind of the four empties by depending upon meditation alone *must* accept an action seal if he or she is to achieve the isolated mind of ultimate example clear light before death.

As has been stated, in order to be successful in practising the meditation with a consort, you must have previously opened your central channel through penetrating the vital points of your own body as explained above. If your central channel has not already been opened in this way, you will be unable to bring the winds into it while embracing a consort. The indication that you have successfully penetrated the vital points of your own body and have caused the winds to enter, abide and dissolve within the central channel is, at the very least, a rough experience of the eight signs from the mirage-like appearance to the clear light. If you have gained such an experience through penetrating the vital points of your own body, you will have no trouble in controlling the winds while meditating with a consort. Therefore, if you are already proficient in controlling your winds through the force of concentration alone, then meditating with a consort can be very beneficial to your practice.

In the *Heruka Root Tantra* there is a detailed explanation of the definition and the different classes of action seal as well as complete instructions as to where, when and how you should enter into that practice so that your winds may be brought into the central channel. According to this root tantra each part of the consort's body should have a specific shape, even including the eyes, the voice should have a certain intonation, and so forth. In addition to having attained a certain level of inner realization, the consort should be skilled in the sixty-four arts of love. Nowadays it is very difficult to find a consort who fulfils all the requirements recommended in this tantra. Therefore, if you yourself have the qualifications mentioned above, you may rely upon a consort that fulfils at least the following minimum requirements. The consort (1) should have some experience of the three principles of the path (renunciation, bodhicitta and the right view of emptiness), (2) should have received the appropriate highest yoga tantra empowerment from a master of secret mantra, (3) should delight in keeping the mantric pledges and (4) should have profound faith in your own spiritual master and personal deity. Finally, if neither you nor your partner have even these minimum qualifications but still wish to practise secret mantra, then during sexual activity you should both try to prevent ordinary appearances from arising, develop the thought of being deities and generate the strong motivation that your intercourse will become the cause of your winds entering, abiding and dissolving into the central channel and thereby lead to the experience of simultaneous great bliss.

As is true for all stages of the sutra and secret mantra paths, it is very important to make constant prayers that you will soon be able to engage in those practices for which you are currently unqualified. If such prayers are made in a heartfelt manner, they will definitely bring about their desired results. Therefore, even before you are fully proficient in a particular practice, you should become familiar with it to the extent of your ability. For example, at the present time you might not be able to generate simultaneous great bliss through practising the eight rounds of inner fire meditation. Nevertheless, if you practise these eight rounds as much as you can then eventually you will gain the actual experience of this meditation. The imprints you have placed upon your mind by attempting the practice will eventually ripen in the form of the desired experience. However, if you are lazy and do not practise at all—and, furthermore, if you do not generate the heartfelt aspiration to be able to practise in the future—you will never attain any realizations or experiences whatsoever.

The practice with the wisdom seal (43)

If you are not yet qualified to embrace an action seal and have not yet met the necessary conditions, you can still practise by visualizing a wisdom seal (jnana mudra). A wisdom seal is a visualized consort and through practising with such a seal, simultaneous great bliss can be generated through the force of visualization and concentration. In this case the wisdom seal takes the place of the action seal. In fact, one of the commitments of having received an empowerment in the mother classifications of secret mantra—for example, the practices of Heruka or Vajrayogini—is to visualize such a wisdom seal three times every morning and three times every evening. Furthermore, if you have sufficient time, when you embrace the wisdom mudra you should melt the white drop in your crown and experience the four joys on the basis of the eight rounds of inner fire meditation described earlier.

Of the three main divisions of the mahamudra that is the union of bliss and emptiness, the first division—generating the subjective simultaneous great bliss—has now been completed.

5 *Introduction to the Nature of Mind*

How to realize the objective emptiness (44)

This, the second main division of the mahamudra that is the union of bliss and emptiness, is explained under three headings:

45 The reason why the intuitive realization of emptiness depends upon the attainment of tranquil abiding meditation

46 The extraordinary methods for attaining tranquil abiding

60 Seeking the view of emptiness from the vantage point of meditation

The reason why the intuitive realization of emptiness depends upon the attainment of tranquil abiding meditation (45)

For the mind to gain an intuitive realization of emptiness it must be able to hold onto its object of meditation without wavering. The ordinary mind, however, because it has not been subdued through the force of tranquil abiding meditation is in constant motion. Conceptual thoughts continuously scatter the mind so that it cannot focus single-pointedly long enough to gain an intuitive realization of anything. Therefore, it is impossible for such a scattered mind to develop a clear perception of a subtle hidden object such as emptiness.

Objects in the field of the five physical sense consciousnesses—sights, sounds, smells and so forth—can be directly perceived without difficulty. Emptiness, however, is classified as a subtle hidden object because, unless one is an enlightened being, such objects cannot be perceived directly by the sense consciousnesses themselves. These so-called hidden objects can initially be known only by the sixth consciousness, that is by mental consciousness. However, because our conceptual mind is unsubdued and in constant motion, it is impossible for this mental consciousness to perceive these subtle hidden objects clearly. As a result the mind does not have the opportunity to mix with these objects and gain an intuitive realization of them.

Tranquil abiding is the name given to that state in which thoughts are no longer able to move and disturb the mind. When such a state of tranquil abiding has been attained, your mind will be able to focus single-pointedly and remain undistractedly for an extended period of time upon any object it chooses—even a subtle hidden object such as emptiness. The longer the mind remains focussed upon its object, the clearer that object will be perceived; as a result eventually you will gain a direct and intuitive realization of that object. Thus it can be seen that the attainment of tranquil abiding, which is in the nature of perfect stillness and unwavering concentration, is an indispensable prerequisite for realizing the subtle hidden object of emptiness intuitively.

Je Tsong-khapa has provided the following analogy to demonstrate the necessity and importance of attaining tranquil abiding of mind. Imagine that you are trying to read a text at night by the light of a candle flame. If a draught is causing the flame to flicker, you will not be able to see the words on the page clearly and therefore you will not be able to absorb their meaning. If the flame is steady, however, you will not have this problem. In the same way, your mind cannot see and understand subtle hidden objects clearly if it is being blown about by the winds of conceptual thought.

Without the attainment of tranquil abiding, your mind will be stubborn and difficult to control; it will not be supple and pliant. You will have trouble focussing upon a wholesome object of meditation and, even if you are able to focus on such an object momentarily, you will be unable to remain concentrated upon it for a long time. Such a mind is like an unsubdued horse over which the rider has no control. It is as if your mind is your master and you are obliged to do as it bids. Its wish—no matter how ill-advised it may be—is your command. Such an unruly mind refuses to engage in those virtuous activities you may wish to perform. If you want to develop concentration, for example, such an unsubdued mind does anything but help. All it does is present hindrances to your practice.

Once you have attained tranquil abiding this situation is reversed. Like a well trained horse, your mind becomes responsive and obedient. Controlled by the reins of mindfulness and alertness, this obedient mind will do whatever you wish. Instead of being an interference, such a well subdued mind will become your greatest helper. With it you will be able to penetrate deeply into whatever object of meditation you choose. And eventually, with the aid of such a mind, you will be able to gain a direct intuitive realization of that most important subtle hidden object: emptiness itself.

Initially it is impossible to realize emptiness intuitively, that is unmixed with a mental image of emptiness. As will be explained below, first you must generate a mental image of emptiness and use that as your object of meditation. Then, as you progress through the stages of tranquil abiding, your realization of emptiness itself will become more and more vivid. Eventually you reach the point where there is no gap between subject (your mind) and object (emptiness itself). When this has been accomplished you have achieved what is known as an intuitive realization of emptiness and have entered the spiritual path of the exalted arya beings, those noble ones who have gained a direct insight into reality.

Why is it necessary to realize emptiness intuitively? The

answer is that without such an intuitive realization you will not only be unable to attain the full enlightenment of a buddha, but you will not even be able to gain the liberation (nirvana) of a lower arhat. Therefore it is not enough simply to realize emptiness; you must realize it intuitively. Furthermore, although tranquil abiding can be attained by using any object of meditation, it is not enough simply to attain this tranquility of mind. If you are intent on travelling the spiritual path to completion your subjective mind of tranquil abiding must have emptiness itself as its object of meditation. Therefore, the most expedient method for reaching the spiritual path of a noble (arya) bodhisattva is to develop bodhicitta and then to attain the tranquil abiding of mind that has emptiness as its object of meditation. If you proceed in this fashion you can annihilate all the obscurations preventing liberation and omniscience, achieve the full enlightenment of a buddha and thereby accomplish your own and others' aims completely.

The extraordinary methods for attaining tranquil abiding (46)
This topic is explained under two headings:

   47 Introduction to the object of meditation: the
         mind itself
   51 The actual meditation on tranquil abiding

Introduction to the object of meditation: the mind itself (47)
According to the system set forth by the masters of the mahamudra lineage, the mind itself should be the object of tranquil abiding meditation. As indicated before, this need not be the only object of such meditation; the *short a* of inner fire can also be chosen. However, whereas the use of the *short a* is peculiar to the practice of secret mantra, the mind itself is used as the object of meditation in both sutra and secret mantra practices.

In general, it is easier to attain tranquil abiding, overcome external distractions and realize emptiness when the mind itself is chosen as the object of meditation. Furthermore, with such an object it is much easier to recognize the nature of the very subtle mind. It is this very subtle mind which goes from life to life. For these reasons, the spiritual masters of the mahamudra lineage have given clear and detailed introductions to the nature of the mind. In general, this is done according to the following method. First the spiritual master explains the attributes of the mind and so forth and tells the disciple how to search for this mind. Then the disciple retires to a place of solitude and meditates according to the instructions received. After some time the disciple returns to the spiritual master and discusses whatever experiences he or she may have had. By means of such a dialogue all misconceptions and incorrect realizations are removed and the disciple eventually gains a perfect understanding and experience. In this manner the gross and subtle minds are revealed and recognized. The doctrine of mahamudra contains very lucid descriptions of the differences between the deceptive or conventional nature of the mind and its ultimate nature as well as detailed explanations of various levels of mind. This is very important because if you lack the experience of the gross mind, you will not be able to know the subtle mind; and if you do not have experience of the subtle mind, you will be unable to know the very subtle mind and will thus be unable to benefit from the clear light experience.

The introduction to the mind is presented in three divisions:

48 The introduction to the general mind
49 The introduction to the individual minds
50 Rejecting the misconception that the deceptive
    or conventional nature of the mind is its
    ultimate nature

The introduction to the general mind (48)

The introduction to the general mind may seem very simple because it is merely concerned with your mind itself. However, you may need some pointing-out instructions to be able to recognize the mind precisely. As there are many disputes among the philosophers as to what the mind actually is, you must make a thorough investigation yourself to ascertain the truth of the matter.

First you should ask yourself, 'Where is my mind located?' In general there are three possible answers to this question. Some people believe the mind is located throughout the body, others that it is located mainly within the heart, while still others believe it exists mainly within the brain. As for the first assertion, there are several good reasons for saying that the mind is located throughout the body. As Aryadeva stated in his *Four Hundred*, all the parts of the body are pervaded by the physical sense faculties and where these faculties exist there are also bodily consciousnesses. When you touch your body you experience a feeling at the point of contact; that feeling itself is mind. Therefore, it can be said that the mind pervades the entire body. You should ask yourself if this is true or not.

There are also good reasons for asserting that the mind is mainly located within the heart centre at the channel-wheel there. This is because the root of the mind—the very subtle mind mounted upon the very subtle wind—resides within this centre. As all gross and subtle minds develop from this subtle mind, it is sensible to assert that the mind is located mainly in the heart centre.

The brain, too, is the site of various sense faculties. Therefore, if someone touches a part of the brain it could produce various feelings and, as stated before, all of these feelings are mind. It is perhaps for this reason that some people claim that the brain is the main location of the mind. If, however, there were no feelings experienced in response to touching the brain, then you would have to conclude that there is no mind in the brain.

The scriptural texts define the mind variously. In some texts the definition of mind is simply that which is clear and cognizing. In others, such as the writings of the Panchen Lama, the definition of the mind is that which is empty of form, cognizes objects and whose nature is clarity. Thus in addition to stating that the mind is clear and cognizing, the Panchen Lama also states that it is empty of form. It is worthwhile to spend a little time analyzing this last point.

Some philosophers assert that the mind *is* physical form. Therefore, when it is stated here that the mind is empty it is refuting that assertion; i.e., to say that the mind is empty in this context means that it lacks or is empty of physical form. There are many ways in which things are said to be empty and it is important to have an accurate idea of what is meant in each case. For example, the sky or space is called empty because it is empty of obstructing contact; it is intangible and does not prevent movement. Yet we can say that the sky has form because when we look at it we see the colour blue. Thus the blue sky does have form but is still empty of obstructing contact. Therefore, though we can say that the mind and the sky are both empty, their objects of negation are different. The sky is called empty because it lacks obstructing contact while the mind is called empty because it lacks form. Therefore, even though the same term is being used in both cases, the denotation of that term varies depending upon what object is being negated. It will be important to keep this distinction in mind later when the much more subtle emptiness of inherent existence is discussed.

When it is said that the mind is empty of physical form, this emptiness does not refer to the ultimate nature of the mind. Rather, it is a description of its conventional reality. Only the mind can be empty of form yet still perceive objects. The mind functions to hold and perceive objects and, while doing so, performs many other functions as well, such as discriminating and experiencing its objects. In summary, it can be said that the function of the mind is to cognize objects. By thinking about the definitions and functions described above, you should be able to obtain a mental image of the mind. Since at present the mind is obscured by dualistic conceptual thought and is therefore difficult to perceive clearly you should strive instead to obtain an accurate mental image of what the mind is. To use an analogous example, although you may not have been to Lhasa you can still obtain a mental image of what Lhasa is like by listening to the tales of an experienced traveller who has been there. Similarly, even though you cannot presently focus upon your mind directly, you can obtain an accurate mental image of what it is like and then meditate upon that mental image. Through the process of engaging in tranquil abiding meditation your gross dualistic conceptual thoughts will gradually die or fade away and you will then be able to perceive the actual object of meditation, in this case the mind itself, very clearly.

Although it was stated previously that the body is pervaded by the mind, it should be understood that if an object is not met with, the mind will not manifest. For example, the direct valid perception by an eye consciousness only arises in dependence upon (1) a visual object and (2) the visual sense faculty, or eye-sensor. If there is a visual object present but no eye sense faculty, then an eye consciousness cannot arise. In the same way, when there is a working eye sense faculty present but no visual object, again it will be impossible for visual consciousness to arise. In short, if the object and sense faculty do not meet, no mind or consciousness will develop. By analogy, if two hands do not meet, there will be no sound of two hands clapping.

The accomplished practitioners of tranquil abiding meditation generally use mind itself as the object of meditation and focus upon the centre of the heart channel-wheel as the precise location of that mind. This very subtle mind residing within the heart is referred to both as the root mind and the resident mind. This latter name is employed to differentiate it from the gross and subtle levels of mind, which are temporary. That is to say, the gross and subtle levels of mind appear and disappear throughout one's lifetime. The very subtle root or resident mind is different for although it also changes from moment to moment, it is constant in the sense that it continues from one life to the next.

Using this very subtle root mind as the object of tranquil abiding meditation is a very powerful technique. This is because in this case the subject is the mind and the object is also the mind. Yet although this meditation can be very blissful and powerful, it can also lead to confusion for those people who are not accustomed to it. For example, meditating in this way you may develop the feeling that there are and must be two different minds: the subjective mind and the objective mind. This uncertainty, however, is only an indication that you are new to this type of meditation. When you become thoroughly familiar with it, you will feel that the subject and object are utterly intermingled.

Meditating that the root mind is located within the heart centre is a very effective method for bringing the winds into the central channel. If you do this meditation within the context of secret mantra practice, you should visualize that the mind is the subtle indestructible mind residing in the centre of the vacuole in the central channel within the heart channel-wheel. As was mentioned earlier, the principal aim of the secret mantra meditator is to develop simultaneous great bliss by bringing the winds into the central channel. Therefore, if at this point you choose the mind itself as the object of tranquil abiding meditation and visualize it as residing within the centre of the heart channel-wheel, you are preparing the way for simultaneous great bliss to arise. When this type of meditation is joined with secret mantra practices, it becomes an indirect completion stage meditation. Thus there are many benefits resulting from choosing the mind itself to be the object of tranquil abiding meditation.

The introduction to the individual minds (49)

According to both sutra and secret mantra the mind can be divided into the primary consciousnesses and the attendant mental factors. In general it is said that there are six of the former and fifty-one of the latter. As these have been extensively explained in many texts already translated into English there is no need to list them here.[13] According to secret mantra there is another way of classifying the various types of mind and this is in terms of their level: gross, subtle and very subtle.

This is the classification that will be dealt with now.

The five physical sense consciousnesses—those of the eye, ear, nose, tongue and body—are necessarily gross levels of mind. The sixth consciousness—mental consciousness itself—has all three divisions of gross, subtle and very subtle. All eighty indicative conceptions listed earlier belong to the gross level of mind. These are the 'used minds' of ordinary beings and include the different thoughts we remember, what we think, all our delusions and so forth. They are 'used minds' because they realize, hold and cognize their objects; they think and meditate and we—the person—use them. In addition, the minds of the first four signs of death and sleep, as well as the same four developed during meditation, are all gross minds. Although the mind of each successive sign is subtler than the mind that preceded it—the mind of the smoke-like appearance is subtler than that of the mirage-like appearance and so forth —all of them are classified as gross because their mounting winds are gross.

Beginning with the fifth sign the subtle minds are experienced. They manifest from the beginning of the mind of white appearance to the end of the mind of black near-attainment. As before, each successive mind is subtler than the last. Each is classified as subtle because during its arisal there are no gross dualistic conceptual thoughts. Finally, after the mind of black near-attainment has ceased, the mind of clear light arises. This is called the very subtle mind because there is no subtler mind than this.[14]

The accomplished completion stage meditator will experience all of these signs while still in the waking state. His or her mind will be gross, subtle or very subtle just as it would be for an ordinary being during sleep or death. The essential point of completion stage meditation is to experience this very subtle mind. Although the clear light mind is a very subtle mind not every very subtle mind is necessarily that of clear light. Why is this so? At the present time all living beings already have a very subtle mind but it is not the clear light. Clear light itself is experienced by ordinary beings only during sleep or their death; it is only the yogis who can experience this mind during meditation as well.

The method for experiencing this very subtle mind receives extensive description in the mahamudra doctrine of secret mantra. Why is this method explained so extensively? The reason is that through this very subtle mind and through its mounted wind one can achieve enlightenment in this very lifetime. The very subtle mind is the substantial cause of the mind of a buddha while the very subtle wind upon which it is mounted is the substantial cause of the form body of a buddha. Without utilizing this very subtle mind and wind there is absolutely no possibility of reaching the perfect enlightenment of buddhahood.

The ability of a mind to function depends upon its mounted wind. If a wind is impure the mind mounted upon it will necessarily be impure as well. On the other hand, if it is a wisdom wind the mind mounted upon it will also be a wisdom mind. Those winds that flow within the right and left channels and those that flow throughout the other 72,000 channels of the body all give rise to dualistic conceptual thought. The winds that flow within the central channel, however, are wisdom winds and they are so-called because the yogis develop their wisdom mind from them. Because all wisdom minds must be mounted upon wisdom winds, it is essential to bring all the winds into the central channel.

According to sutra, self-grasping (Skt. atmagraha; Tib. dagdzin) is the root of samsara and all its suffering. Thus the methods explained in sutra for gaining release from suffering deal only with overcoming this self-grasping mind. According to secret mantra, however, not only self-grasping but the impure winds themselves are called the root of samsara. Thus the doctrine of secret mantra not only explains how to overcome self-grasping but also how to overcome the impure winds upon which it is mounted. When this is done there is release from cyclic existence. Because the methods taught in secret mantra overcome not only self-grasping but also the impure winds, they are considered superior to those of sutra.

Although you may not be able to practise the superior methods of secret mantra at this moment, you should make the firm determination to practise them in the future. When you consider how rare the true secret mantra teachings are—as Je Tsong-khapa has stated, they are even rarer than the buddhas—you should feel very joyful that you now have the opportunity to study these precious teachings. The more you understand and appreciate the good fortune of having met these teachings and the more you pray to be able to put them into practice in the future for the benefit of others, the quicker you will achieve actual success through these methods.

Rejecting the misconception that the deceptive or conventional nature of the mind is its ultimate nature (50)

Some mahamudra instructors and practitioners assert that when the clarity and cognition of the mind are directly perceived without the veil of conceptualizations, then the meditator has realized the emptiness that is the ultimate nature of the mind. They claim that this clarity and cognition is the mind's ultimate nature and the students of such instructors also fall into this mistaken view. This misconception arises from the fact that those who hold this wrong belief do not understand the perfect view as it was explained by Nagarjuna. They do not properly understand what ultimate true nature means and, if asked what the ultimate nature of the mind is, they cannot establish it as being a non-affirming negation. They think the ultimate nature of the mind is its clarity and cognition free of conceptualization; they do not realize that the ultimate nature of the mind is the non-affirming negation that is the mere absence of the inherent existence of the mind. This mere absence of inherent existence is very subtle and therefore quite difficult to comprehend. The clarity and cognition of the mind, however, is not nearly as subtle and thus relatively easy to understand. This is one reason why meditators can hold onto erroneous beliefs concerning the ultimate nature of the mind.

According to the *Perfection of Wisdom Sutras* and the

view of Nagarjuna, real emptiness is the mere absence of inherent existence. For this reason it is called a non-affirming negation. Those who do not understand the subtlety of this view are unable to see any difference between such a non-affirming negation and utter non-existence. For this reason they make mistakes when trying to understand the ultimate nature of the mind. They assert that a non-affirming negation does not exist at all and therefore reject the views of Nagarjuna and the *Perfection of Wisdom Sutras*. Instead, when they meditate merely upon the clarity and cognition of the mind and experience these very vividly, they think they are realizing the emptiness that is the ultimate true nature of the mind. The emptiness that they are experiencing, however, is merely the lack of physical form and the freedom from conceptualization; it is not the emptiness of inherent existence.

The First Panchen Lama, Losang Chökyi Gyaltsen, soundly refuted this misconception. In his commentary on mahamudra practice he wrote:

> The mind that is free from conceptualization
> Is merely a level of deceptive mind;
> It is not the mind's ultimate nature.
> Therefore seek instruction from qualified masters.

Thus the Panchen Lama is clearly stating that what some meditators take to be the ultimate nature of the mind—its clarity and cognition—is merely the mind's deceptive or conventional nature.

If you mistakenly believe this deceptive nature of the mind to be its ultimate nature, you may easily develop distorted pride and many other related faults. This can happen as follows. When, through meditation, you gain a vivid perception of the mind's clarity and cognition, you will feel that you have gained an intuitive realization of emptiness, that you are beholding it directly. And, as it is possible to develop a slightly blissful feeling from such a meditation, you may conclude, 'Now I have developed the simultaneous great bliss of secret mantra.' Afterwards you might come to think, 'Now I have developed the mahamudra that is the union of simultaneous great bliss and emptiness.' There is the chance that through the force of further meditation you might become free for a short while from conceptual thought. Then it is possible to develop the distorted pride that thinks, 'Now I am free from the two obscurations; now I have become a buddha.' Of course this attainment has not been reached at all. Inevitably you will have to confront those circumstantial conditions— such as an object of anger or attachment—that give rise to the various deluded states of mind. It will then become evident that the 'enlightenment' you experienced was only illusory. All of these mistakes come from misunderstanding the ultimate nature of the mind because you did not follow the instructions of qualified teachers or did not study such instructions completely.

In general the First Panchen Lama, although he was in fact a very highly realized practitioner, behaved in a very humble manner. But when writing about the necessity of refuting mistaken and misleading teachings be boldly stated:

> As we cannot perceive the mindstream of others
> We should strive to appreciate the teachings of all;
> But I cannot accept those who spread wrong views
> And through those wrong views lead many astray.

What the Panchen Lama wrote several hundred years ago is particularly applicable today. If the pure dharma is to flourish in western countries, it is absolutely essential that one's beliefs be thoroughly checked and stand in accordance with the pure teachings of Buddha Shakyamuni. The ugly, unfortunate result of not understanding the pure dharma and of following misleading teachings which pretend to be the pure dharma is sectarianism. This is one of the greatest hindrances to the flourishing of the dharma, especially in the West. Thus anything that gives rise to such an evil, destructive mind should be eliminated as quickly and as thoroughly as possible.

Nowadays there is a very strong tendency to believe without

the slightest hesitation every word spoken by someone of high reputation. A humble practitioner giving perfect and accurate teachings is often neither appreciated nor believed. Shakyamuni Buddha himself cautioned his disciples against adopting such a mistaken attitude by stating, 'Do not accept my teachings simply because I am called Buddha.' Time and time again he reminded his disciples not to accept his teachings out of blind faith but to test them as thoroughly as they would assay gold. It is only on the basis of valid reasons and personal experience that one should accept the teachings of anyone, including Buddha himself.

In the teachings on the so-called 'four reliances' Buddha gave further guidelines for achieving an unmistaken understanding of the teachings. He stated:

(1) Do not rely upon the person, but upon the dharma.
(2) Do not rely upon the words, but upon the meaning.
(3) Do not rely upon the interpretative meaning, but upon the definitive one.
(4) Do not rely upon consciousness, but upon wisdom.

These lines can be explained as follows. (1) When deciding which doctrine to rely upon, do not be satisfied with the fame of a particular teacher. Instead, investigate his or her teachings themselves. Upon investigation if you find these teachings reasonable, perfect, faultless, then you should accept them. If they are opposite to this then you should reject them, no matter how famous or charismatic their expounder might be. Furthermore, (2) you should not be satisfied with the mere poetry or the beautiful rhetoric of a particular set of teachings. Only if the meaning of the words is reasonable should you rely upon and accept them. In addition, (3) you should not be satisfied merely with an interpretative meaning of conventional or deceptive truth but should rely upon and accept the definite meaning of the ultimate truth of emptiness. In other words, because the wisdom teachings of emptiness and the method teachings of bodhicitta and so forth are companions, you should not be satisfied with only one or the other but should practise them jointly. Finally, (4) you should not be satisfied with impure, deceptive states of consciousness, but place your reliance upon the wisdom of an arya being's meditative equipoise.

If you understand these four reliances and use them to evaluate the truth of whatever teachings you might receive, you will be following an unmistaken path. There will be no danger of adopting false views or falling under the influence of misleading teachers. You will be able to discriminate correctly between what is to be accepted and what is to be rejected and will thereby be protected against such faults as sectarianism.

Je Tsong- khapa

6 Tranquil Abiding

The actual meditation on tranquil abiding (51)
   This major topic is explained in three parts:

   52 Maintaining tranquil abiding meditation
      through general mindfulness
   53 Maintaining tranquil abiding meditation
      through individual types of mindfulness
   59 Maintaining tranquil abiding meditation
      through the six methods of settling the mind

*Maintaining tranquil abiding meditation through general
mindfulness* (52)
   If tranquil abiding is to be attained it is very important to
remove all the obstacles interfering with it and to gather all the
elements that enhance it. Therefore, in this section dealing
with general mindfulness there will be a discussion of the obstacles preventing successful tranquil abiding meditation and
the opponent forces employed to overcome these obstacles.
   The first obstacle to tranquil abiding meditation is laziness.
The three types of laziness are indolence, discouragement and
attraction to what is negative. The laziness of indolence refers
to the complacent attitude in which you are content with
samsara and therefore do not generate the perseverance to go

beyond this unsatisfactory state of existence. Under the influence of such laziness you lack the energy to rouse yourself from lethargy. The laziness of discouragement arises from believing you lack the ability to engage in a particular virtuous or wholesome action. For example, if you think that the attainment of tranquil abiding is totally beyond your capability you will easily become discouraged from practising this form of meditation. Finally, the laziness of being attracted to what is negative refers to expending your energies in inappropriate areas. With such laziness you are happy to indulge in worldly activities but lack all interest in, or are even displeased with those wholesome activities leading to a cessation of suffering. All these forms of laziness block the gate to the kingdom of tranquil abiding thereby preventing you from entering this powerful and elevated state of mind.

The four remedies to laziness are faith, aspiration, joyous effort and suppleness. The first two combat laziness indirectly while the last two are direct opponents. Faith in tranquil abiding is gained by contemplating its manifold benefits. Then, on the basis of such faith, you aspire to attain the actual state of tranquil abiding and this aspiration leads inevitably to joyous effort. With joyous effort you overcome the laziness of indolence and through your enthusiastic practice gradually attain the mental suppleness that cuts the very root of laziness so that it does not arise ever again.

Thinking about the benefits of tranquil abiding meditation is an effective way of ridding yourself of whatever laziness may be interrupting your practice. One of the advantages of this type of meditation is that through it, it is possible to achieve such heightened states of consciousness as telepathy and so forth. Why is it important to gain such powers of mind? Because without them you will be very limited in your ability to help others. For example, it often happens that despite our compassionate intentions we inadvertently bring harm to others. We may give advice out of a pure motivation to benefit someone, yet this advice—because it is not based upon a clear perception of the total situation—may actually lead the other person astray. With telepathy and other powers of heightened awareness, however, such problems do not arise.

One example of the benefits of developing telepathy and so forth comes from the biography of the great meditator Asanga. On one occasion he was giving a public discourse and in the audience was a very powerful king. This king decided to test Asanga's authenticity and so he formulated in his mind three difficult questions concerning the *Perfection of Wisdom Sutras*. Through the powers he had gained from tranquil abiding meditation Asanga was able to read the questions within the king's mind and answer them perfectly during his discourse. This display of power and insight so impressed the king that he developed great faith in Asanga and his teachings and, as a result, the dharma was able to flourish throughout his realm.

As indicated, laziness is a general obstacle to successful dharma practice. When one is engaged in tranquil abiding meditation itself, there are three more specific obstacles to be abandoned: mental wandering, mental excitement and mental sinking. As these three are the worst hindrances to the attainment of tranquil abiding, it is essential that you recognize them clearly and then apply the appropriate remedies. Just as it is necessary to know who your enemy is before you can stop him from harming you, in the same way you must be able to recognize all three obstacles before you can keep them from interfering with your meditation. Furthermore, it is not enough to have mere intellectual knowledge of these hindrances; you must know them from your own personal experience. Only then is it possible to destroy them completely. As it is difficult to distinguish between a proper and a flawed state of concentration, you should rely upon accurate and detailed teachings that point out clearly even the most subtle hindrance interfering with perfect meditation. Such flawless instructions can be found, among other places, in the writings of Je Tsong-khapa and his followers. Therefore, if possible, you should study these texts thoroughly.

The first obstacle to be recognized is mental wandering.

This can occur while you are focussed on any wholesome object of tranquil abiding meditation. If, in such a state, your mind moves to any object other than an object of attachment, it is said you have fallen under the influence of mental wandering. For example, if you are meditating upon the figure of Shakyamuni Buddha and your mind moves to the form of Avalokiteshvara or Tara then, even though these are also wholesome objects, your mind has succumbed to mental wandering. There are two degrees of such wandering, the subtle and the gross. If your mind moves to the other object slightly without losing the original object of meditation, this is subtle mental wandering. However, if the mind moves to such an extent that the original object of meditation is lost completely, gross mental wandering has occurred.

The next obstacle is mental excitement. This also occurs while your mind is fixed upon any wholesome object of tranquil abiding meditation. If your mind wanders to an object of attachment, this is termed mental excitement. An example would be trying to develop tranquil abiding by meditating upon the figure of a buddha and having your mind move to a memory of your boyfriend or girlfriend. If your mind wanders to such an object of attachment slightly without losing the original object of meditation, this is subtle mental excitement. Such subtle mental excitement does not break the thread of your meditation for it is like a small fish that can swim back and forth without disturbing the water. If your mind is affected by gross mental excitement, however, the original object of meditation is totally lost because you have become completely involved with an object of attachment.

Mental wandering and excitement are relatively easy to recognize. It is much more difficult to recognize mental sinking, especially in its subtle form. If your mind is focussed upon a wholesome object of tranquil abiding meditation and either the clarity of that object or the intensity with which your mind holds that object decreases, then mental sinking has occurred. For example, if you are meditating upon the *short a* of inner fire and either the clarity of this letter decreases or the intensity with which you hold onto it decreases, then your concentration has given way to mental sinking. As was the case for mental wandering and excitement, mental sinking is of two types: subtle and gross. If the intensity with which you hold your object of meditation decreases slightly, this is an instance of subtle mental sinking. If both the intensity and the clarity decrease then gross mental sinking has occurred.

These hindrances of mental wandering, excitement and sinking constitute the obstacles to be overcome by tranquil abiding meditation. The etymology of tranquil abiding is as follows: 'tranquil' refers to the pacification of the distracting minds and 'abiding' refers to the mind's ability to remain upon the chosen object of meditation single-pointedly. Therefore, the proper way to approach the tranquil abiding meditation is to begin by sitting in the proper meditation posture, make sure you do not have a dull or sleepy mind and then try to overcome the negative conceptualizing minds that are drawn towards external objects.

The latter point can be elaborated upon as follows. It is very important to be able to discriminate between the defiled and the clear mind. This is analogous to the importance of discriminating between dirty and clean drinking water. If you want to drink from a mountain stream, you do not do so from the turbulent part because the water there will be mixed with dirt and silt. Rather you drink from a calm part of the stream where the water is clean and clear. In the same way, it is necessary to overcome and avoid the various distracted minds, which are like turbulent water, so that you can drink deeply from the clarity of the calm and peaceful mind.

The recommended method for pacifying the turbulent distracted mind is to begin your meditation session by expelling the impure winds. This was explained in the first of the eight rounds of inner fire meditation. Once you have done this and your mind has reached an acceptable level of calmness, you should try to recall the pointing-out instructions concerning the meditation object given to you by your spiritual master.

This activity is called 'seeking the object of meditation'. This will eventually lead you to a correct mental image of the object which in this case is the mind itself; this is known as 'finding the object of meditation'. The next activity is called 'holding the object of meditation'; once you have found the correct mental image you should endeavour to hold on to it without forgetting. The fourth and final activity is called 'remaining on the object of meditation' which involves focussing upon the held mental image with strong single-pointed concentration. These four activities of seeking, finding, holding and remaining on the object of meditation are of extreme importance in the development of true concentration and will be discussed again below.

It is a great shame not to know what concentration actually is. True concentration must have two characteristics: (1) holding the object through the force of intensified mindfulness and (2) remaining single-pointedly upon that object. Any mind that has these two characteristics is flawless concentration. When meditating you should examine your mind to see if it is endowed with these two qualities. It is much better to spend a short time in true concentration than to spend a long time in faulty practice.

Concerning the obstacles to proper meditation, it is relatively simple to identify mental wandering and excitement and to see how they are hindrances to your attainment of tranquil abiding. However, it takes an experienced meditator to recognize subtle mental sinking and distinguish it from true single-pointed concentration. If you are unable to distinguish these two, there is the danger that your concentration will become mixed with subtle mental sinking. If this happens your meditation will yield negative results. Therefore, to safe-guard against this fault you must utilize the faculty of discriminating alertness from time to time. While the main portion of your mind is focussed upon the object of meditation, a corner of the mind should check to see if wandering, excitement, sinking or any other fault is arising. Such discriminating alertness is a form of analytical wisdom.

It can also happen that suddenly you forget what the object of meditation is. To safe-guard against this hindrance you should be very mindful of the object of meditation from the very beginning of your session. This will help to prevent your memory of this object from degenerating. Thus it is clear that mindfulness is of central importance in single-pointed concentration meditation. When there is strong mindfulness it is very hard for wandering, excitement and sinking to arise. To keep strong mindfulness of the meditation object you should use the following two methods: (1) make a strong determination to maintain an unbroken mindfulness throughout the meditation session and (2) when you recognize that it is about to degenerate, intensify your mindfulness before this degeneration actually takes place. Mindfulness is the very life of meditation and is said to have three functions: (1) not forgetting the meditation object, (2) holding onto this object and (3) overcoming distractions.

In summary, by destroying sinking, excitement and wandering through the force of mindfulness and discriminating alertness you will be able to attain a state of tranquil abiding. Allowing these faults to remain in your mind without trying to overcome them is known as 'non-application' and is a great hindrance to proper meditation. It should be eliminated by a conscientious application of the appropriate opponent forces whenever faults arise in the mind during your meditation session. Such application naturally follows from maintaining at all times a strong intention to accomplish the aims of your practice. Therefore, you should keep these aims foremost in your mind, remember how tranquil abiding allows you to achieve these aims and be determined not to let laziness or any other delusion keep you from your goal.

In order to achieve a perfect state of tranquil abiding you must progress through nine stages of development. These nine stages, as well as the eight opponents to the five obstacles, the four attentions, the six forces and so forth, have been explained in great detail in other texts and if you are interested in developing deep concentration you should become familiar with these explanations.[15] Here, however, and in the following sections a brief description of each stage of mental development will be given to demonstrate how general and individual mindfulness help bring the mind to a state of perfect tranquil abiding.

The first two stages of mental development are called *placing the mind* and *continual placement* respectively. They are attained through the force of general mindfulness in the following manner. At the beginning of your meditation session after you have assumed a comfortable posture on your meditation cushion, you should go through the four steps of seeking, finding, holding onto and remaining focussed single-pointedly upon the object of meditation: your mind itself. As explained before, you need to use general mindfulness to remember the pointing-out instructions that enable you to gain a correct mental image without forgetting it.

At the beginning it will be very difficult to remain in single-pointed concentration upon the object for any significant amount of time. Much effort must be used merely to search for and find the object and even when it is found there will be difficulties in retaining hold on this object. Therefore, it is helpful to think of your meditation session as divided into many sub-sections. Having gone through the four steps of concentration and then losing the object of meditation, you should consider that the first sub-section of your session has come to an end. Begin the second sub-section by immediately seeking and then finding the object again and then engage in holding and remaining as before. Each time you lose the object, abandon that sub-section and move to the next.

It is said that at the beginning it is good to have eighteen such sub-sections during each meditation session. However, this is just general advice; you can do more or less than this recommended amount as you see fit. Furthermore, it is unnecessary to interrupt your attempts at concentration by keeping an exact count of how many sub-sections you are doing; an approximation is good enough. The idea is to be as alert and mindful as possible at all times, checking the quality of your concentration, noting whenever you have lost the object and then immediately beginning the next sub-section.

At the first stage, called *placing the mind*, you will barely be able to hold onto the meditation object before losing it. Again and again you will have to seek and find the object and take hold of it. Eventually, however you will be able to remain focussed on this object for up to five minutes without losing it. When you are able to do this you have reached the second stage: *continual placement*.

When you first start to practise tranquil abiding meditation you may devote only an hour or less to such practices, but eventually you should be doing from four to six sessions a day. Building up your practice in such a gradual manner is the best way to proceed. As stated before, it is better to do a short meditation with your concentration keen than a long one with it faulty.

This concludes the discussion of general mindfulness. The seven remaining stages of mental development are developed by depending upon individual mindfulness and will therefore be discussed in the following sections.

Maintaining tranquil abiding meditation through individual types of mindfulness (53)
This is explained according to the following five divisions:

54 Meditating on tranquil abiding by means of new mindfulness
55 Meditating on tranquil abiding by means of old mindfulness
56 Meditating on tranquil abiding by means of appropriate methods
57 Meditating on tranquil abiding by means of labels used by others
58 Meditating on tranquil abiding by means of overcoming conceptual thoughts

Meditating on tranquil abiding by means of new mindfulness (54)
During the first two stages of development, each time you

lose the object of meditation you have to search for it again, find it, hold onto it and then remain on it single-pointedly. Thus even though you are constantly renewing your mindfulness, this renewed mindfulness cannot take hold of its object immediately. At the third stage of development, however, your familiarity with the object has developed to the point where you can re-establish your hold on the object immediately after losing it; there is no longer any need to seek it. Therefore, the mindfulness employed to bring your mind back to its object is now called 'new' mindfulness and this third stage of development is appropriately called *replacement*.

While on the third stage you are still bothered by distractions that, like a thief, can steal away your attention. Thus you must continually apprehend this thief, remove him and then return your mind once more to the meditation object. In comparison to the first two stages, at this third stage of mental development your mind can be returned to its object very quickly by means of new mindfulness.

Meditating on tranquil abiding by means of old mindfulness (55)

At the third stage of mental development you had to employ new mindfulness again and again because the mind kept losing its object of meditation. Eventually, the point is reached where you are able to hold onto this object without ever having to employ new mindfulness. In other words, from the beginning to the end of the meditation session you can hold onto the meditation object without ever breaking the continuity of your concentration. Gaining such an ability is the sign that you have achieved the fourth stage of development, called *close placement*. Because at this stage your mindfulness does not degenerate once it has been set, it is said that you are now maintaining your meditation by means of 'old' mindfulness. Through the power of such old mindfulness you are able to cut the distracted conceptualizing mind without ever forgetting the object of meditation.

An analogy taken from the *Basket of Discipline* is used to demonstrate the importance of maintaining unbroken concentration by means of old mindfulness. A duel is being fought between two enemies: one is an archer and the other bears a sword-wheel which he spins like an aeroplane propeller. As long as he continues to spin his weapon, none of the archer's arrows can ever harm him for they are all sliced to pieces by the whirling blades. Thus the duel goes on and on and the archer is never able to penetrate his opponent's defence.

Finally the wife of the archer, a woman of great beauty, formulates a clever plan. She tells her husband that when the duel continues she will attire herself in seductive clothing and stand in the opponent's line of vision. This she does and when the opponent is distracted by desire and momentarily forgets to spin his sword-wheel, the archer seizes the opportunity and slays him with an arrow. With his dying breath the opponent declares, 'It was not the archer who has killed me but my own lack of mindfulness.'

In the same way that the undistracted sword-wheel bearer kept his weapon spinning, so should you maintain your tranquil abiding meditation by means of old mindfulness; you should destroy all conceptual thoughts with one continuous mindfulness without interrupting your concentration upon the meditation object. When, at the fourth stage of development, you are able to accomplish this, you have completed the full power of mindfulness. It should be noted, however, that a skilful practitioner will not have very long meditation sessions at this fourth stage. Because sinking and excitement still occur at this stage, it is not wise to meditate uninterruptedly for long periods of time; this would only further engrain bad habits.

Meditating on tranquil abiding by means of appropriate methods (56)

At the fourth stage of development, the power of mindfulness is completed and you have the ability to remain on the meditation object uninterruptedly throughout the session. However, the excessive effort needed to maintain this unbroken level of concentration will cause the mind to become too collected, and subtle sinking will arise. Thus on the fifth stage—called *controlled mind*—it is necessary to apply the power of discriminating alertness in order to uplift the mind. You need to relax slightly the effort of maintaining concentration yet still be able to remain single-pointedly upon the meditation object.

At this point it is possible for a mistake to arise. The instruction to relax does *not* mean that after holding and remaining on the meditation object you should loosen your grip on the object itself. At this stage that would be a grave error. It is true that the great mahasiddha Saraha said that if one completely relaxes, tranquil abiding will certainly be attained. However, his remarks were meant for those at the eighth and ninth level of development, not for those still at the fifth. At this stage it is not your concentration that should be relaxed but rather the effort used to overcome the faults of sinking and excitement. If this effort is not relaxed slightly, you will develop distractions and thereby interfere with your concentration.

If you are able to hold onto the meditation object and yet relax the effort needed to maintain single-pointed concentration on it, you are maintaining tranquil abiding meditation by means of appropriate methods. In other words you are applying effort appropriately, to the exact degree required. To do this properly, however, requires a great deal of practice. Even the great Indian meditator Chandragomin declared, 'When I depend upon effort, mental excitement occurs; but when I abandon that effort sinking sets in.'

It is important for a meditator interested in developing tranquil abiding to gain a deep understanding of these points. Such an understanding, however, will not grow from mere intellectual familiarity with the teachings. Rather, you must gain personal experience of all the nine stages of mental development by actually putting these and other instructions into practice. This is the only way progress can be made.

Once you reach the fifth stage of mental development your concentration is strong and stable and it is definite that you will achieve tranquil abiding if you continue to apply effort in meditation. On your way to this goal you pass through the remaining four stages of development, which can be briefly explained as follows.

At the sixth stage, known as *pacified mind*, you complete the power of discriminating alertness. Although at this stage there is no more danger of subtle sinking, there is great danger of subtle excitement. This is because on the fifth stage the meditator was uplifting the mind. Through the force of alertness this subtle excitement can be easily overcome.

On the seventh stage one's balance cannot be upset by subtle sinking or excitement because the powers of mindfulness and discriminating alertness are now complete. Although they may possibly arise, the meditator can overcome them immediately with effort. This stage is known as *complete pacification*.

At the eighth stage, known as *single pointedness*, it is impossible for sinking and excitement to develop. Here it requires only a little effort to remain focussed upon the meditation object for the entire session without experiencing even the slightest interruption to concentration.

Finally on the ninth stage known as *balanced placement* or placing the mind on the object with equanimity, without effort one is able to maintain faultless concentration. You have become so completely familiar with the object of meditation that it requires no effort at all to remain focussed upon it single-pointedly.

Meditating on tranquil abiding by means of labels used by others (57)

The maintenance of tranquil abiding meditation in relation to mahamudra has been described in terms of three labels: abiding, moving and mixing. However, different meditators at different times have used these same three labels to refer to different states of meditation. Therefore, to avoid confusion, these varying usages should be differentiated from one another.

Some of the early mahamudra meditators have asserted that *abiding* refers to remaining single-pointedly upon the held object of meditation, *moving* to the arisal of conceptual thoughts while still remaining on the object and *mixing* to the dissolution of these conceptual thoughts back into the root mind, which is the object of mahamudra meditation. These early mahamudra meditators state that it is very important and also very difficult to recognize these three states well and clearly.

Some later mahamudra scriptures mention the same three states of meditation with the same three labels, but assert that it is not very difficult to recognize them. According to the analogy of a pond, *abiding* corresponds to the water's being still and clear, *moving* to the formation on the bottom of bubbles and their arising, while *mixing* corresponds to the bursting of these bubbles and their dissolving back into the water.

Both the earlier and later mahamudra meditators agree that during the state of abiding you should strive not to develop any conceptual thoughts at all. However, if they should arise, then you should make an effort to dissolve them back into the root mind; this is the practice of mixing. As for the contradiction between the assertions that the recognition of these three states is difficult or easy, this is only an apparent contradiction. The earlier meditators are stressing that it is difficult to recognize these three states *through experience*, which is certainly true for beginners while the later meditators are stressing that it is not difficult to differentiate these three states *intellectually*. This is one possible solution to the apparent contradiction.

Still other mahamudra meditators give another interpretation of these three labels. Some of the later mahamudra meditators state that *abiding* refers to the immutable tranquil abiding meditation, *moving* to the wisdom of superior insight meditation and *mixing* to the union of these two. They use the analogy of a goldfish swimming in a perfectly still and clear pond to illustrate their meaning. Tranquil abiding is like the still and clear pond while superior insight is like the goldfish swimming in this pond. The state of union, or mixing, corresponds to the stillness of the water even though the fish is swimming about in it. Therefore, in the state of true union, the functioning of wisdom does not in any way upset the tranquility of the fully concentrated mind. Tranquil abiding, superior insight and the union of these two are the main abiding, moving and mixing of mahamudra meditation.

Meditating on tranquil abiding by means of overcoming conceptual thoughts (58)

The mahasiddha Saraha used the following example to clarify the meaning of this form of tranquil abiding meditation. When merchants sail to a far-away land to conduct their business, they take a crow along with them to help judge how far they are from their destination. When they think they might be near their goal, they release the crow. It flies high into the sky looking for a dry place to land but, if there is none to be found, it returns to the ship because there is no other place to alight.

The ship is analogous to the mind itself: the object of mahamudra tranquil abiding meditation, while the flight of the crow corresponds to the arisal and movement of conceptual thought. Just as the merchants free the crow to fly, so should the meditator allow whatever conceptual thoughts that develop during tranquil abiding meditation to arise and wander as they will. However, with a part of your mind you should watch this wandering conceptual thought, in the same way that the merchants observe the flight of the crow. After a while this wandering thought will eventually rejoin the meditation object, the mind itself, in the same way that a crow far out at sea must eventually return to the ship. All wandering conceptual thoughts must return to the main meditation object for the simple reason that all thoughts initially arise and finally dissolve back into the mind itself. Meditating in this way, therefore, is the means to overcome conceptual thought.

This concludes the fifth and last sub-division of the second section dealing with tranquil abiding meditation: maintenance by means of individual types of mindfulness.

Maintaining tranquil abiding meditation through the six methods of settling the mind (59)

The explanation given in the previous section on the general and individual types of mindfulness contain detailed instructions on the methods for fixing the mind on the object of meditation, avoiding the faults and obstacles interfering with your meditation and achieving full tranquil abiding of mind. What follow are six examples, drawn from instructions by the great Saraha, that illustrate the best frame of mind to be cultivated for anyone wishing to achieve such tranquil abiding. They have been included here because it is felt that these examples might be especially helpful to contemporary meditators.

(1) *The sun unobscured by clouds.* Just as the sun is unmixed and unobscured by clouds, your meditation should be unobscured by and unmixed with all the obstructions to perfect concentration, such as distracting conceptual thoughts, mental sinking and so forth.

(2) *The flight of the garuda bird.* As this most powerful bird circles in the air, it maintains its smooth glide by occasionally shifting the angle of its wings. This it does with just the right amount of effort; it never adjusts its flight in a violent or frantic manner. Similarly, when practising tranquil abiding meditation with your mind fixed single-pointedly upon the meditation object, you should employ just the right amount of effort to keep your concentration balanced. If you use too much effort you will experience distraction, while if you use too little you will succumb to mental sinking.

(3) *The stillness of an ocean without waves.* When there are no waves and no wind blowing, the ocean remains unmoving. In the same way, when your mind has been freed from the waves of distraction, you should remain on the meditation object single-pointedly without any mental movement.

(4) *A small child looking at temple murals.* When a child is looking at the various works of art decorating the walls of a temple, he or she is satisfied with a superficial perusal of them. In a similar fashion, someone who is unfamiliar with

tranquil abiding meditation should, in the beginning, be satisfied with a rough perception of the object of meditation. Striving to gain too detailed or clear a vision at first will cause many distractions to arise and eventually the object will be lost completely. Later, however, when you have grown familiar with the object, you can try to gain a more exact image of it in the same way that an adult looking at temple murals will study them in the most minute detail.

(5) *A bird leaving no trail behind it as it flies.* Because a bird leaves no tracks in the sky when it flies, no one would think of following such a non-existent trail. Similarly, during meditation bird-like thoughts may arise in the mind, but you should not let yourself follow after such thoughts. Instead, place your mind on the object of meditation—the mind itself—and have it remain there single-pointedly.

(6) *The best quality cotton thread.* Cotton thread of the highest quality has two attributes: in addition to being soft and smooth it is very strong. During tranquil abiding meditation your mind should possess similar qualities. Like the soft and smooth thread it should be comfortable and relaxed, yet it should be strongly tied to the object of meditation by means of mindfulness.

If your practice of tranquil abiding meditation follows the instructions given above you will progress naturally through all nine stages of mental development. As far as these stages are concerned, once you have attained the first three you will be able to pass through the remainder without difficulty. The achievement of each stage depends on mastering the one before it; therefore, a steady, gradual, step-by-step practice is the best one to follow.

After the ninth stage of development has been attained and you can remain focussed effortlessly and unwaveringly on the object of meditation, there are various states of mental and physical suppleness and bliss through which you will pass before the actual state of tranquil abiding is reached. This process can be described as follows.

On the ninth stage the meditator will experience a very special and beneficial wind flowing throughout the crown channel-wheel. The movement of this wind will bring about a great *mental suppleness* and your mind will become free of all discomfort, extremely flexible and delighted to engage in any wholesome activity whatsoever. Then this wind will flow throughout your body, bringing with it great *physical suppleness*. A body possessing such physical suppleness is very agile and comfortable and delights in the performance of wholesome actions. Such a body seems very light and the meditator will almost feel able to fly. This experience of lightness and freedom will induce a strong feeling of intense *bliss of physical suppleness* and as a result of experiencing this blissful feeling in the body the mind itself will attain immutable *bliss of mental suppleness*. Once this mental bliss has been achieved, the meditator will have reached the actual state of tranquil abiding. This state possesses such extra-ordinary clarity of mind that the meditator will feel as though he or she could count all the atoms of the world.

Such a mind of tranquil abiding is no longer a mind of the desire realm. Your concentration has become so powerful that all appearances other than that of the object of meditation will completely vanish while you are engaged in actual placement meditation. Because the mind is the meditation object in mahamudra practice, when you enter into concentration you will perceive nothing but your mind itself. You will feel that your physical body has vanished and you will abide within the blissful nature of your mind, free from any external appearance or internal conceptual thought.

When you arise from the formal placement meditation and enter the period known as subsequent realization or post-meditation, you will again perceive the ordinary appearances of the sense world. However, because of your previous experiences, it will be very difficult to become drawn to beautiful objects of attachment or repulsed by ugly objects of aversion. Even if attacked it will be very difficult for anger to arise. In the same manner, the other poisons of jealousy and so forth will lose their power to pollute your mind. Having achieved unshakeable control over the mind, you will have gained dominance over delusion through the sheer force of concentration.

While it is true that you now have the power to keep the delusions from arising in your mind, you still have to cut the root of these delusions. This is accomplished only when you have gained an intuitive realization of emptiness: the ultimate nature of reality. However, with the single-pointed concentration gained through tranquil abiding meditation you now have the ability to gain deep understanding of whatever object you place before your mind. Therefore, if emptiness becomes the object of your concentration during placement meditation, you will easily be able to gain a profound realization of it and thereby sever the root of all poisonous delusions. You will be able to perceive emptiness with great clarity and penetration because your mind has achieved freedom from all the distractions of conceptual thought.

There are, in general, two paths you can take after achieving tranquil abiding: the mundane and supramundane. Through following the former you can attain super-normal powers such as clairvoyance, the ability to perform so-called miracles, rebirth in the god realms and so forth. Although these attainments are remarkable, they are insignificant in comparison with the results of following the supramundane path. Through traversing the latter you can reach complete personal liberation and the full enlightenment of buddhahood. If, for example, you have developed renunciation—the thought definitely to emerge from cyclic existence—and your mind of tranquil abiding meditation meditates continuously on the emptiness of inherent existence, you will eventually achieve arhatship, or nirvana. And if this mind of tranquil abiding possesses not only renunciation but in addition meditates on the various mahayana practices, you will be able to remove even the subtlest mental obscuration and thereby attain buddhahood. As the practice of mahamudra is a mahayana one, the path to be taken is the supramundane. Therefore, once tranquil abiding has been attained it must be used to develop and complete the realizations of renunciation, bodhicitta and the correct view of emptiness. The meditation on emptiness will be explained in the next chapter.

7 Meditation on Emptiness

Seeking the view of emptiness from the vantage point of meditation (60)

This section has three sub-divisions:

61 The way to meditate upon the selflessness of persons

68 The way to meditate upon the selflessness of other phenomena

69 The necessity of following the works of Nagarjuna for those wishing to realize the right view of emptiness through the path of sutra or of secret mantra

The way to meditate upon the selflessness of persons (61)

This first sub-division is divided into three sections:

62 The essential point of recognizing the object of negation

63 The way to reject the object of negation

67 How to sustain the selflessness that is the emptiness of the object of negation in the states of both meditative equipoise and subsequent realization

The essential point of recognizing the object of negation (62)

Recognizing the object of negation is essential if emptiness, the ultimate nature of reality, is to be realized. Although people often speak about emptiness, it cannot be realized until the object of negation is clearly identified. The many misconceptions about emptiness arise mainly because this object of negation has not been properly understood. What is the object of negation? In this case it is the independent, self-existent 'I'. Other terms to refer to this self-existent 'I' include the inherently existent 'I', the naturally existent 'I', the truly existent 'I', the 'I' that exists from its own side and the 'I' that exists in its own right.

Such an independent, self-existent 'I' must first be identified and then rejected. How does this 'I' exist? The answer is that this 'I' *has never existed at all*. If it did actually exist then it would not be a proper object to reject or deny. This is a very important point to understand; the self-existent 'I' referred to in emptiness meditation is totally false and non-existent. By rejecting or denying it, therefore, you will not be destroying something that actually exists; rather you will be gaining a deep understanding that, despite mistaken beliefs, such an 'I' never existed in the first place.

At this point a grave doubt may arise: 'If the self or the "I" that is the object of negation does not really exist, then how can it appear to the mind at all?' To answer this doubt you must realize that although something may appear to the mind, this is *not* a sufficient reason to say that it really exists. The existence of something cannot be validated simply on the grounds that it has appeared to the mind. For example, consider the experience of someone with faulty vision who seems to see hair falling in front of his or her eyes. Actually there is no hair falling, yet it still appears to someone whose vision is impaired. By thinking about examples such as this you will be able to understand how the self-existent 'I' can appear to the mind and still be utterly non-existent.

In order to realize emptiness—which is the rejection of the object of negation—you must obtain a clear and vivid mental image of the self-existent 'I' as it appears to the mind. When you first do such an investigation you should not think that this 'I' does not really exist; instead merely try to perceive it as clearly as possible. The following instructions may be helpful in this regard.

There are two types of 'I': one has never really existed at all (the so-called self-existent 'I') and the other is the 'I' that actually exists. The actual 'I' is merely imputed by thought and any 'I' that is *not* merely imputed by thought is the self-existent 'I', the object of negation. Therefore, when you are trying to gain a clear mental image of the 'I' to be rejected you should seek the 'I' that is not merely imputed by thought; you should look for the one that appears to exist in its own right.

When you first sit down to do mahamudra emptiness meditation, you should make the strong determination to recognize the self-existent 'I'. Then you should invoke this 'I' and hold it tightly, allowing the mind that thinks in terms of this 'I' to arise. You can do this easily by imagining that you are falling from a high place, by remembering the harsh words that were addressed to you by another or by any other similarly provocative means. When you do this the self-existent 'I' will arise vividly and you should then observe how it appears to the mind. In this case the mind that holds on to the 'I' is the subject, or subjective mind, while the self-existent 'I' itself is the object held by that subjective mind. The object and the object-holder will appear as two separate entities; on this side you have the object-holder, which is the subjective mind, and on that side you will have the held object, which is the 'I' itself. This 'I' will naturally appear to the mind as if it were independent, existing from its own side and in its own right without depending at all on the subjective mind. This is so because the 'I' that appears is the independent, self-existent 'I'.

When you have clearly perceived the 'I' that seems to be an object not depending upon the subjective mind, you have found the object of negation. Apart from this there is no other self-existent 'I'. Whenever you perceive an 'I' that does not depend upon the subjective mind you are recognizing the object of negation and you should therefore try to perceive this 'I' as clearly as possible.

Having recognized the object of negation you should not immediately reject it. You should continue your meditation by thinking, 'This is the very "I" that I had always thought existed; this is what I have cherished and protected since beginningless time.' When someone speaks harshly to you and you feel, '*I* have been insulted; how dare he say that to *me*,' it is this 'I' that you are thinking about. At the moment of insult you perceive only this 'I' and think, 'He spoke to *me* very badly,' subsequently becoming angry. On such an occasion you never perceive the 'I' that is merely imputed by thought. In fact, until you have gained an experience of emptiness, whenever you think about or refer to yourself you are holding onto the self-existent 'I', the very object of negation in emptiness meditation.

Having brought this self-existent 'I' to mind in this manner you should think, 'Until now I have believed that this "I" really existed and therefore have cherished and protected it. However, I have never investigated whether this "I" actually exists or not.' You may have heard someone give a discourse on emptiness or have read the buddhist philosophical literature that states that this 'I' does not exist, but this is not enough. Now you should generate the strong intention to discover the truth for yourself. The way to investigate whether this 'I' actually exists or not is to perform the logical analysis explained in the next section.

The way to reject the object of negation (63)

This analysis is made up of three parts:

64 The essential point of ascertaining pervasion
65 The essential point of ascertaining the absence of singularity
66 The essential point of ascertaining the absence of plurality

Upon the basis of investigating these three essential points you will be able to reject completely the independent, self-existent 'I' that appears so vividly to the mind.

The essential point of ascertaining pervasion (64)

There are both a general and a specific explanation of this essential point. In general, when someone is talking about an object of knowledge—something that can be validly known—there are only two possible types of things being referred to. Either that person is talking about one single object (a man, an army, etc.) or about a combination of two or more objects (a man and wife; Tom, Dick and Harry, etc.). Therefore, although there are countless objects of knowledge, all are pervaded by or included within one of two categories: the singular or the plural. In other words, if something really exists, it must necessarily be one or more than one. There is no third possibility. This is the general explanation of ascertaining pervasion.

In the specific explanation the object dealt with is the independent, self-existent 'I'. It is this 'I' that we are going to investigate and if it exists it must be either a singularity or a plurality. To be more exact, this 'I' must be either one with the aggregates (of body and mind) or different from these aggregates. There is no third manner in which this 'I' can exist. To understand the meaning of this essential point requires grasping the deep significance of what is implied by the concept of pervasion.

The essential point of ascertaining the absence of singularity (65)

There are many mistakes that follow if you consider the 'I' to be one with the aggregates. For example, just as there are five aggregates there would have to be five 'I's. Or, just as the 'I' is one, the five aggregates must also be one and the same. Both of these conclusions are obviously wrong. On the basis of such an investigation, therefore, you can realize that the 'I' is not one with the aggregates.

The essential point of ascertaining the absence of plurality (66)

Having seen that the 'I' is not one with the aggregates, check to see if it could possibly be separate. However, if it were separate, you could find this 'I' after removing all the aggregates and could think 'I' even if they were non-existent. This is impossible.

Furthermore, if the 'I' were separate from the aggregates then when you become sick there would be no reason to say, 'I am sick.' In actuality it is the aggregate of form that is sick; therefore it would be much more appropriate to say, 'My body is sick.' And if you were dying there would be no reason to think, 'I am dying' but rather, 'My body is dying.' This can be understood by thinking of the following example. When a cow is dying you never generate the thought, 'A horse is dying' because a cow and a horse are totally separate entities. Following the same line of reasoning, if the 'I' and the aggregates are separate then why should someone think, 'I am dying' when actually it is only the aggregates that are passing away. To use another example, if a person's body is beautiful he or she will say, 'I am beautiful.' However, if the 'I' and the body (one of the aggregates) are different, what is the point in saying, '*I* am beautiful'? By thinking of incorrect consequences such as this you will be able to realize that the 'I' cannot be different from the aggregates. You will thereby be able to ascertain the absence of plurality: the third essential point in refuting the object of negation.

When you have established that the 'I' cannot exist as one with nor separate from the five aggregates you will realize that the object of negation, the self-existent 'I', does not exist at all. You will have realized the non-self-existence of the 'I'. You should decide that the self-existent 'I' which does not depend upon the aggregates does not exist at all. Having discovered this you should meditate that such an 'I' is totally non-existent. At this point you have found the emptiness which is the negation of the 'I' existing from its own side. Such an emptiness should be taken as the object of your meditation.

In the beginning, meditation upon emptiness should be done only for a short period of time. Gradually, as your familiarity grows, you can extend the time spent in this meditation. Through the force of this practice you will come to feel that the 'I' that was developed before doing this meditation upon emptiness is lost. You will perceive and feel that the 'I' you have cherished will also be lost. It will also occur to you that the 'I' that you apprehended so strongly does not exist at all. If and when all this happens you will have received a slight experience of emptiness.

The following example illustrates how you should think when you arise from emptiness meditation. It is evening and in the shadow of your room you think you see a scorpion. Believing that this dangerous animal is really in your room you generate strong fear. Then you turn on the light and look in the place where you thought you saw the scorpion. After making a complete search, however, you discover that in reality there was no scorpion there at all. All you find is a small piece of wood; the scorpion you saw before was nothing but an hallucination, a product of your imagination.

There are many points of similarity between the events just described and the process of searching for the self-existent 'I'. To begin with, the scorpion you thought you saw and the independent, truly existent 'I' are very much the same. Furthermore, the thought that clings to the supposed existence of the scorpion is like the self-grasping mind that clings to the existence of the independent 'I'. In addition there is a similarity between the bases upon which the mistakes were made, that is between the piece of wood in the shadows and the aggregates of mind and body. Also, thinking that there is a scorpion in the room and feeling fear is similar to the fear of cyclic existence that arises from grasping onto a self-existent 'I'. The search to see whether there really is a scorpion in the room or not and the investigation to see whether the self-existent 'I' really exists or not are also similar. The understanding, upon investigation, that there is no scorpion in the room is similar to the understanding that there is no self-existent 'I'. And finally, the disappearance of your fear when you realize that the scorpion is non-existent is similar to the way that all your fears will eventually disappear after you have meditated continuously on the non-existence of the self-existent 'I'. Using an example like this is very beneficial for your practice. By thinking about this illustration and its meaning you should try to reach the realization that your 'I' does not exist from its own side.

In general, all the things that appear to the ordinary mind seem to exist from their own side. It is for this reason that the highest buddhist school, the Prasangika, states that all of the minds of ordinary beings are mistaken cognitions. Whatever appears to an ordinary being's mind appears to exist from its own side and not as merely imputed by thought. It is this persistent mistake that is responsible for all suffering and dissatisfaction and it is this same mistake that is rectified by meditation upon emptiness.

It sometimes happens that through the force of meditating upon your 'I' as being empty of inherent self-existence you will feel that you are losing your 'I' completely. If this happens it is very possible that you will experience some fear. This should not be considered as something bad or as a mistake: such a feeling of fear is a sign that you have gained a slight experience of this meditation. For example, the great lama Je Tsong-khapa was once giving a discourse on emptiness to more than a thousand disciples. One of these was the accomplished meditator Je Sherab Sengge who, during the discourse, had the strong experience that his 'I' did not exist from its own side. Feeling that his 'I' was lost, he developed some fear and responded by suddenly grasping on to the edge of his upper garment and clinging to it. He did this instinctively to remind himself of the existence of the conventional 'I', the 'I' that is imputed by thought. With his clairvoyance, Je Tsong-khapa realized that his disciple had developed the experience of emptiness and praised him accordingly. Therefore, it is not necessarily a bad sign for fear to arise during emptiness meditation. In general, however, when you realize that there is no self-existent 'I', there is no more reason to feel any fear at all. As Shantideva wrote in his *Guide to the*

Bodhisattva's Way of Life:

> If there were a truly existent 'I'
> It would be right to develop fear towards any
> object.
> But since there is no truly existent 'I' at all
> Who is there to be afraid?

Some people may find that the explanation given here differs from other explanations of the object of negation. It may even appear to contradict them. If such a doubt arises it can only be removed by discussing it with those who are experienced in emptiness meditation. It is difficult to eradicate such doubts merely through the written word.

How to sustain the selflessness that is the emptiness of the object of negation in the states of both meditative equipoise and subsequent realization (67)

As explained, the object of negation in emptiness meditation is the self-existent 'I'. During the sessions in which you are developing meditative equipoise you should focus your mind upon this 'I' and generate the following thought: 'Up until now I have always believed this "I" to exist. However, as a result of the previous line of reasoning (the meditation upon the three essential points) I have discovered that this "I" is completely non-existent.' By the force of first focussing your mind upon the object of negation and then becoming convinced of its complete non-existence you will perceive an emptiness like that of space. This space-like emptiness is the emptiness or lack of self-existence (true existence, inherent existence, natural existence, etc.) and becomes the object of your meditation. As is the case with other objects of meditation you should hold onto this emptiness without forgetting it and remain focussed upon it single-pointedly. If you meditate upon emptiness with a mind that has achieved complete tranquil abiding, your realization of emptiness will become clearer and clearer. Eventually you will be able to realize emptiness—the mere rejection of the object of negation—intuitively. When this direct, non-conceptual realization of emptiness has been gained, you will have gone beyond the state of ordinary beings. You will have achieved the path of the noble superior ones: the glorious arya beings.

The next phase of meditation is known as the state of subsequent realization. It occurs after you have arisen from your meditative equipoise upon space-like emptiness. If this meditative equipoise—which is maintained by focussing upon the mere absence of the self-existent 'I'—is practised well during the placement meditation session, then the illusion-like yoga of subsequent realization will go well during the post-meditation period.

During the space-like equipoise you should strongly abandon the notion of a self-existent 'I'. During the time of subsequent realization, however, the 'I' will reappear as if it were truly existent from its own side. This happens because your mind has been strongly conditioned by its beginningless belief in self-existence. Despite this strong conditioning, a concentration developed during equipoise will enable you to realize that although the 'I' again *appears* to exist truly and self-existently, it does not actually do so. Thus, the re-appearance of the self-existent 'I' during the subsequent realization period is perceived in the same way that a magician perceives his own creation. Although he sees the things that he has magically produced, he does not believe in the authenticity of what appears. He knows that this appearance is merely an illusion. Likewise, if you have meditated well on space-like emptiness in the state of equipoise then even though the self-existent 'I' will subsequently appear to you, you will be able to think that such an 'I' does not really exist. You will be able to consider the 'I' to be like an illusion. This thought that the 'I' is like an illusion should not be forgotten at any time.

If during your session of meditative equipoise you have strongly abandoned the self-existent 'I', then in the subsequent realization stage you will have a very distinct and special feeling. For example, normally if someone bothers you, the thought arises in your mind, 'That person is abusing *me!*' As explained before, the 'I' or 'me' that appears to the mind at this time is the 'I' that appears to be truly self-existent. However, if your space-like meditation has been successful, you will not fall into the trap of identifying with such a truly-existent 'I'. You will be able to think, 'Why should I become upset? This "I" does not truly exist.'

Becoming upset upon receiving abuse and the like is a sign that you are identifying with the self-existent or truly-existent 'I'. At that time you perceive a very independent 'I' that does not depend upon your body and mind. If this 'I' has been rejected strongly during space-like meditative equipoise, then you will not hold onto it firmly when it reappears during the subsequent realization stage. By loosening your grip on such an 'I' you will automatically be able to dispel fear, anxiety, frustration and all other unhappy states of mind.

According to the experience gained in meditative equipoise you discover that the idea, 'He hurt and abused me' is wrong because the object of that idea—the independent, truly-existent 'I'—has been found to be utterly non-existent. At this point a strong doubt or contradiction may arise in your mind: 'To think that person has *not* in fact harmed me would contradict what everyone would agree has actually happened. It goes against the normal, conventional way of thinking and speaking. Therefore, how can it be correct?'

Sensing such a contradiction is not bad; it is an indication that you have contemplated emptiness well. The only reason this contradiction arises is that you have failed to understand the conventional 'I'. Thus this contradiction can surely be dispelled if you make a strong effort to comprehend how the 'I' exists conventionally.

You must understand that this conventional 'I' is not the 'I' that was the object of negation. What will you eventually perceive by following a qualified spiritual master and analyzing how the 'I' exists conventionally? You will feel that you have to remain satisfied with the mere *name* of 'I'. You will be able to make the firm decision, 'I must engage in all activities being satisfied merely with this name or label.' Once this experience has been achieved immutably, you will have gained the deep realization of the subtle conventional 'I'. At such a time you will have understood that the 'I' exists merely by being imputed by the mind. Then, on the basis of such an understanding, you will be able to determine confidently that there is no contradiction between the thoughts: 'The "I" is empty of true, inherent self-existence' and 'The "I" merely exists conventionally.' You will be able to dispel your previous confusion concerning the invalidity of the thought, 'He abused me' because you will have discovered the view that is the union of the two truths: ultimate and conventional.

The way to meditate upon the selflessness of other phenomena (68)

Not only is your sense of 'I' empty of independent, self-existence, so too are all other phenomena. Take the example of your physical body. If, for instance, you are experiencing physical weakness you think, 'My body is weak.' It does not occur to you to think, 'My arms and my legs are weak' or 'My head is weak' or 'My trunk is weak.' Instead, you perceive a vividly appearing 'body' that is completely independent of these six 'limbs' of arms, legs, head and trunk. If such a body actually existed in the way it appears, it would be a self-existent or truly-existent body. This, however, is the object to be negated although it is normally believed to exist.

First you should try to perceive this vividly appearing body as clearly as possible; try to discern the normal attitude you have about such a body. Once this has been done you should think, 'Up until now I have believed such a body to exist and therefore I have cherished it. But now I am no longer satisfied with merely believing that it exists; I will investigate for myself and find out whether it does or not.'

The next point to decide is that this truly-existent body, if it really does exist, must be somewhere within the six limbs or somewhere apart from them. There is no other possibility. So begin your search within each of the six. Upon investigation it will be discovered that none of the limbs taken separately is this body (e.g. 'My arm is not my body') nor is the collection of these six the body.

It is easy to see how the individual limbs are not your body, but it requires deeper thought to realize why the collection of these limbs is not your body either. The collection of the six limbs is, in actuality, the basis upon which your body is imputed. Your body is an imputed phenomenon, imputed in dependence upon this collection of six limbs. Thus the collection itself is not the body (neither the truly-existent nor the conventional one) but rather the basis upon which the body depends. If this mere collection of limbs were the body, then it would absurdly follow that the body depends on the body; in this case one body would become two. Because you obviously do not have two bodies, the mere collection of limbs cannot be the body for which you are searching.

Following such an investigation you are able to conclude that neither the individual limbs nor the collection of these limbs is the body. Furthermore, if you check somewhere else other than these two alternatives for the vividly-appearing body you will not able to find it anywhere. As a result you will be able to reject the object of negation—the appearance of a body that is unrelated to its parts—because, upon close investigation, such a body remains unfound.

As a consequence of your investigation the only thing you will perceive is the emptiness that is the absence or negation of the truly-existent body. Taking this emptiness as your object of meditation, focus your mind upon it without forgetting. If you can do this single-pointedly, your meditation will become the space-like equipoise on the body's being empty of true existence. Then, during the subsequent realization period when you are no longer focussed single-pointedly upon this emptiness and the body reappears, you should regard your body as an illusion. The way of seeing it as an illusion and the way of understanding how your body exists merely conventionally can be known through the previous explanation of the selflessness of persons.

If, by using perfect reasons and examples, you know how your 'I' and your body are each empty of natural, inherent, true, self-existence, you can apply the same approach to other persons, your mind and all other phenomena. In this way you

will come to realize that everything lacks self-existence and is
only a mere imputation by conceptual thought.

This has been merely a brief discussion of emptiness
meditation. For more detailed explanations you should consult those texts—such as the sixth chapter of Chandrakirti's
Guide to the Middle Way and the ninth chapter of Shantideva's
Guide to the Bodhisattva's Way of Life—where the correct view
of emptiness is elucidated.[16] However, it is not enough merely
to study such texts. You must depend upon the advice of experienced guides—fully qualified spiritual masters—and meditate according to their instructions. Only in this way will your
doubts be removed and will it be possible to gain a deep insight into the ultimate nature of reality.

*The necessity of following the works of Nagarjuna for those
wishing to realize the right view of emptiness through the path of
sutra or of secret mantra* (69)

That all phenomena without exception are empty of inherent or natural existence is the view of the incomparable
Middle Way Consequentialists (Madhyamika-Prasangika) as
well as being the ultimate intention of Buddha himself as expounded in his *Perfection of Wisdom* teachings. The wisdom of
emptiness is the ultimate view in the systems of both sutra and
secret mantra and thus is essential to all paths leading to
liberation and full enlightenment.

Emptiness is a subtle topic and is only truly understood by
those with great wisdom. Beings who are weak-minded will
have much difficulty merely in recognizing the correct object
of negation. One of the main contributions made by the
glorious Nagarjuna was his explanation of the actual intended
meaning of Buddha's wisdom teachings. In his extensive
writings, Nagarjuna explained clearly and exactly what it is
that phenomena are empty of, thereby explaining the meaning
of emptiness itself.

Such explanations are necessary because the *Perfection of
Wisdom* teachings themselves can be misinterpreted. For
example, these teachings state, 'Form is empty of form; sound

is empty of sound' and so forth. Because the intended meaning of such statements is not easily understood, many people have developed incorrect notions of what they signify. They mistakenly interpret such statements to mean that form is not form or that form does not exist. As explained by Nagarjuna, however, the actual intended meaning is that form is empty of *truly-existent* form. Thus emptiness does not connote utter non-existence, as some would assert, but rather the absence of inherent existence: the completely fallacious mode of existence mistakenly believed in by the ignorantly-conditioned mind. It is the wisdom of emptiness that eradicates such ignorance and leads one to complete liberation from the fears and sufferings of cyclic existence.

There are four major traditions of the Buddhism of Tibet— the Nying-ma, Sa-kya, Ka-gyu and Ge-luk—and from the beginning the realized masters of all of them have adhered to the Middle Way Consequentialist system of Nagarjuna. For example, one of the most sublime of all Nying-ma spiritual masters was Long-chen Rab-jam-pa (1308-1364). In his *Commentary to the Treasury of Instruction* he states that Buddha's ultimate intention was explained by the glorious Nagarjuna. He also states that Buddha himself predicted in *The Great Drum Sutra* that Nagarjuna would come to this world and expound this ultimate view. Of the many followers of Nagarjuna it was Chandrakirti, the main propagator of the Middle Way Consequentialist system, who interpreted Nagarjuna faultlessly, and Long-chen-pa himself followed Chandrakirti's view. Therefore, if someone is a pure Nying-ma practitioner, that person must adhere to the view of Nagarjuna in the same way that Long-chen-pa and indeed the great Padmasambhava did.

The outstanding Sa-kya masters of the past also adhered to the view of Nagarjuna. For example, when the great Ngor-chen Kun-ga Zang-po (1382-1457) was asked about the different philosophical views he answered, 'I don't know about the different views; I only studied Nagarjuna's view of the Middle Way. That is my own view because it is the essence of the dharma.' Many other Sa-kya masters, such as the Venerable Ren-dawa (1349-1412) also held the same view. Therefore, if someone is a pure Sa-kya practitioner, that person must adhere to the view of Nagarjuna.

The great Ka-gyu masters also followed the Middle Way Consequentialist view as is clearly seen in the songs of Milarepa (1052-1135) and in the *Jewel Ornament of Liberation* by Gampopa (1079-1135). Je Tsong-khapa (1357-1419), founder of the Ge-luk tradition, also expounded this view and wrote many texts commenting upon Nagarjuna's work. Thus if someone is a pure Ka-gyu or Ge-luk practitioner that person must also adhere to the view of Nagarjuna.

Besides these four schools there was also the tradition of Kadam meditators in the lineage of the Indian master Atisha (982-1054). Atisha stated that Nagarjuna's view was flawlessly expounded by Chandrakirti and that this is the only view that will lead one to buddhahood. In fact, if someone holds a view that is contrary to Nagarjuna's, there is no chance of reaching enlightenment no matter how much that person meditates. When his Tibetan disciple Drom-ton-pa (1005-1064) offered his experience of emptiness to his spiritual master, Atisha replied, 'You have made me very happy; you have found the view of Nagarjuna.'

Some people mistakenly think that there is a special view of emptiness presented in secret mantra, but this is not true. As the Sa-kya Pandita (1182-1251) said, 'There is no difference in the view of emptiness between sutra and secret mantra.' Therefore, if a practitioner is sincerely interested in travelling the path to enlightenment, he or she must make a concerted effort to understand the view of Nagarjuna and train in the wisdom realizing the emptiness of true, inherent self-existence.

With this discussion of objection emptiness the first major division of mahamudra—the mahamudra that is the union of bliss and emptiness—is completed.

8 The Illusory Body

There are five divisions or separate stages of completion stage practice and all are contained within mahamudra meditation. These five are generally listed as (1) isolated speech, (2) isolated mind, (3) illusory body, (4) clear light and (5) union. This last-named stage is also called the union needing practice and it must be attained if you wish to accomplish the union that does not need practice: buddhahood itself. Because each of these stages depends on the one before it, you must practise all five if you want to reach enlightenment quickly.

It should be noted that according to another listing there are six stages of completion stage practice, beginning with what is known as the isolated body. Just as there is an isolated body practice of the generation stage, which is a yoga that overcomes the appearance of the ordinary body, so too is there a similar, but more advanced, isolated body practice of the completion stage. Success in the latter depends on having practised the earlier generation stage yoga.

According to this system of mahamudra, whatever meditations you do on the yoga of inner fire after you have attained the isolated body of the completion stage are included within the yoga of the isolated speech. The main purpose of the meditation on the isolated speech is to loosen or untie the channel knots of the heart. As explained earlier, when these

Je Phabong-khapa

knots are untied and the winds enter, abide and dissolve within the central channel at the level of the heart, the meditator experiences the four empties. A mind experiencing any of these empties through the force of such meditation is called an isolated mind because it is isolated from ordinary dualistic appearances and gross conceptual thought. This summarizes the first two divisions of completion stage practice.

The mahamudra that is the union of the two truths (70)

This is divided into three sections corresponding to the remaining three divisions of completion stage practice:

71 The explanation of the stages for attaining the deceptive illusory body
76 The explanation of the stages for attaining the ultimate clear light
80 The actual explanation of the mahamudra that is the union of the two truths

The explanation of the stages for attaining the deceptive illusory body (71)

This is divided into four headings:

72 Requesting the qualified spiritual master to explain the instructions concerning the illusory body
73 The necessity of depending upon these instructions for those wishing to know the precise meaning of the illusory body
74 Recognizing the basis for attaining the illusory body
75 The explanation of the actual method to attain the illusory body

Requesting the qualified spiritual master to explain the instructions concerning the illusory body (72)

The illusory body is of utmost importance in the practice of secret mantra and should only be explained to qualified disciples. In his *Five Stages of the Completion Stage* Nagarjuna listed the four attributes such a disciple should possess. He or she (1) should have received the empowerments of highest yoga tantra and have experience of the generation stage, (2) should be training in and practising the true meaning of secret mantra and have the experience of the discriminating wisdom that clearly discerns and comprehends this true meaning, (3) should be engaged in the practice and have experience of the isolations of body, speech and mind of the completion stage and finally (4) must have strong appreciation of and devotional faith in the deceptive illusory body, in the ultimate clear light and in the mahamudra that is the union of these two truths. Once the qualified disciple has reached the realization of isolation of mind and is in a position to attain quickly the isolated mind of ultimate example clear light—directly after which the impure body will be attained—he or she should request and then receive from the spiritual master instructions on this illusory body. This is important because the manner of achieving this body is very subtle and the disciple must therefore depend upon a fully qualified teacher.

If the illusory body could only be explained to disciples with the above-mentioned attributes there might be very few people qualified to hear about it. Therefore, you should at least have the following four attributes that are similar to the ones mentioned by Nagarjuna. That is you must (1) have received the highest yoga tantra empowerments and be training and practising the generation stage, (2) have the wisdom to understand the true meaning of the secret mantra texts, (3) be trained in and practising the three isolations of the completion stage and especially (4) have strong appreciation for and devotion in the illusory body, clear light and union of these two truths. Those who have either the actual or approximate attributes are qualified to request the spiritual master to expound upon the illusory body and it is permissable for the master to explain them.

Chandrakirti's *Clear Lamp of the Five Stages* and Nagarjuna's *Five Stages of the Completion Stage* explain how a disciple should request these teachings. He or she should first make prostrations to the spiritual master and then present mandala and other offerings. Finally, he or she should make the actual request for the explanation of the illusory body.

It is very important, both in this situation and in general, to be skilful in the way you ask questions of your spiritual master. If they are clear and precise, your doubts can be removed instantly. Because the illusory body is such a subtle subject it is often difficult for the ordinary disciple to ask about it clearly. Therefore, in his *Lamp of Condensed Deeds* Aryadeva explained how these questions should be put. In the example that follows notice how the disciple begins by stating what he or she already knows about the subject and only then poses the actual questions. The disciple approaches the spiritual master and says, 'The practice of secret mantra began with the generation stage where the ordinary appearances of myself and of all other phenomena were prevented from arising. This was done by generating myself in the form of the deity and visualizing the entire phenomenal universe as this deity's mandala. But this practice of deity yoga was merely visualized or imagined; I did not actually attain the body of the deity. Furthermore when I generated myself as this deity during the isolations of body, speech and mind practised on the completion stage, I did not achieve the actual body of the deity either but only an imagined one. The actual body of the deity is only gained when I achieve the illusory body. This is the wisdom body adorned with the thirty-two noble symbols and eighty noble examples of a fully enlightened being. Therefore, please tell me: When is the actual body of the deity—the illusory body—achieved? What is the nature of this body? What is the basis for attaining it? How is it attained? What are its excellences and so forth?' This is the skilful way of questioning your spiritual master.

The necessity of depending upon these instructions for those wishing to know the precise meaning of the illusory body (73)

In Chandrakirti's *Clear Lamp of the Five Stages*, which is a commentary to Nagarjuna's *Five Stages of the Completion Stage*, he lists the four attributes of the illusory body and also states that such a body is attained through depending upon the instructions of a qualified master of secret mantra. As for the four attributes, the illusory body is (1) free from any type of ordinary appearance, (2) perceived only by the meditator himself and those who have also attained the illusory body, (3) not an object realized by logicians who do not practise and (4) the actual body of the deity adorned with the thirty-two noble symbols and eighty noble examples. As for the instructions of a qualified master, these refer to the explanation contained in Nagarjuna's *Five Stages*, Aryadeva's *Condensed Deeds* and Chandrakirti's *Clear Lamp*. Without following the instructions set forth in these three texts there is no way for you to know the illusory body through your own experience.

The method for attaining the illusory body was initially set forth by Vajradhara in the *Guhyasamaja Root Tantra*. Because the words of this tantra are so-called vajra words they are very difficult to comprehend. They require accurate explanation by a qualified teacher to be intelligible and it is just such an explanation that Nagarjuna, Aryadeva and Chandrakirti provide in their works. Whatever was difficult to understand in Nagarjuna's text was clarified by Aryadeva and Chandrakirti in their commentaries. Furthermore, the explanations of all three were synthesized into a single set of instructions by Je Tsongkhapa in his *Lamp of Clarity of the Five Stages of the Completion Stage*. An additional advantage of Je Tsongkhapa's synthesis is that it dispels the misconceptions about the completion stage practices that arose when various scholars misinterpreted the Indian pandits.

Nagarjuna stated that if one does not realize the illusory body then there is no purpose in studying or practising either sutra or secret mantra. He said this because buddhahood—the ultimate goal of all study and practice—cannot possibly be attained unless you achieve the illusory body. To become a buddha you must attain a buddha's form body and the illusory body is its primary or substantial cause. Without the primary cause for a sprout—which is the seed of that sprout—no amount of earth, moisture, sunlight or fertilizer will yield the desired result. In the same way, no matter how much you might study and meditate upon the teachings of sutra and secret mantra, if you do not attain the illusory body it will be impossible to reach buddhahood. However, once you do actually attain the illusory body it is definite that you shall reach perfect buddhahood within that very lifetime. But to attain this body you must rely upon the instructions of a qualified master. Why is this?

According to the perfection vehicle of mahayana (i.e. the sutra path), a bodhisattva on the tenth and final ground (bhumi) is a very highly realized being and is on the verge of attaining perfect buddhahood. According to secret mantra, however, such a bodhisattva—though highly realized—is far from the attainment of buddhahood when compared with the secret mantra meditator who has gained the illusory body. This is because he or she still lacks the prerequisites for achieving enlightenment, specifically the illusory body, which can only be attained through the practice of highest yoga tantra and in reliance upon the instructions of a vajra master. If this is true for a bodhisattva on the tenth ground, then how much more true it must be for the arhats of the two lower vehicles (shravaka and pratyeka-buddha). In addition to the bodhisattva of the perfection vehicle and the practitioners of the two lower vehicles, there are others who do not follow highest yoga tantra, namely those engaged only in the practice of the three lower classes of tantra. None of these practitioners, no matter how advanced they might be, can attain the illusory body because it is only in the system of highest yoga tantra that this illusory body is expounded.

Even though a practitioner may study the highest yoga tantra teachings, it is still necessary to depend upon the instructions of a vajra master. There are two divisions of highest yoga tantra: mother and father, and it is in the latter—particularly in the *Guhyasamaja Root Tantra*—that the illusory body is principally explained. The *Guhyasamaja Tantra* is like a treasury filled with precious jewels—such as the explanation of the illusory body, the vajra recitation and much more—but if you wish to use these jewels for your benefit you must first obtain the key to the treasury. This key is provided by the texts of Nagarjuna, Aryadeva and Chandrakirti; but that is still not enough. Even if you were able to read these texts by yourself you would still have great difficulty in understanding their meaning. Even these texts require interpretation and this is provided by the vajra master.

Consider the following example. In his *Five Stages* Nagarjuna states, 'The illusory body dwells within your body; it is because of your lack of good fortune that you do not comprehend this.' If this literal statement is not explained there is the danger of misinterpretation and resulting mistakes in practice and so forth. If the illusory body actually existed within your body already—as the mere words of this quotation imply—it would not be necessary to follow the path of dharma at all. Therefore, this cannot be Nagarjuna's intended meaning. As Je Tsong-khapa explained, Nagarjuna meant that the *seed* of the illusory body exists within all living beings; it is their lack of accumulated merit that prevents them from cultivating what is potentially within them at the present moment.

This is only a minor example but it shows how necessary it is to rely on a qualified vajra master. It is not enough to gain an intellectual understanding of highest yoga tantra; your mind must absorb and become united with its actual intended meaning. Thus the instructions you receive must have been handed down through an unbroken succession of masters that can be traced back through your personal spiritual mentor to Buddha Vajradhara himself. It is absolutely essential that you receive the appropriate empowerments as well as the verbal instructions from such a fully qualified vajra master.

Just as the union of simultaneous great bliss and emptiness is one of the quickest and most important paths to buddhahood, so too is the illusory body. However, it is much more difficult to know why this is true of the illusory body than it is to know why it is true of that union. This is a further reason why it is essential to rely on the instructions of a vajra master.

The function of the union of simultaneous great bliss and emptiness is to destroy the obscurations preventing omniscience very quickly. The ability to do this depends upon the illusory body because, if the union of simultaneous great bliss and emptiness is to destroy these obscurations quickly, a great deal of meritorious power must be accumulated. Such an accumulation is completed through the force of attaining the illusory body. According to sutra, merit has to be collected by following pure bodhisattva conduct for three countless great aeons before enlightenment can be attained. In secret mantra, however, these aeons of merit can be accumulated in one lifetime by meditating upon the illusory body.

As stated in Chandrakirti's *Guide to the Middle Way*, anything that principally assists in the attainment of a buddha's holy form body is called the accumulation of merit, while anything principally assisting in the attainment of a buddha's holy truth body is the accumulation of wisdom. In secret mantra, the method to accumulate the greatest amount of merit in the shortest amount of time is through meditating upon the illusory body and the way to accumulate wisdom as speedily is through the union of simultaneous great bliss and emptiness.

Both sutra and secret mantra agree that the attainment of buddhahood depends upon the completion of these two collections of wisdom and merit. The difference is that in sutra it is impossible to meditate on the practice of these two accumulations simultaneously within one single thought. While engaged in the practice of accumulating merit you cannot at the same time be accumulating wisdom with one mind. And when you are single-pointedly meditating upon emptiness you cannot simultaneously be accumulating merit. There is no practice of the inseparability of method and wisdom in one sutra meditation. In secret mantra, however, when the mind of simultaneous great bliss fixes upon emptiness single-pointedly, you are accumulating both merit and wisdom at the same time. Such a meditation comprises both method and wisdom, and the inseparability of these two in one meditation is what makes secret mantra the swift path to enlightenment.

Recognizing the basis for attaining the illusory body (74)

The illusory body is defined as the actual body of the deity, which develops from the subtle wind upon which is mounted either the isolated mind of ultimate example clear light or the mind of meaning clear light, and adorned with the thirty-two noble symbols and eighty noble examples. That which develops from the wind mounted by the example clear light is called the impure illusory body, while the one that develops from the wind mounted by the meaning clear light is called the pure illusory body.

Here the difference between pure and impure is determined by whether the mounting clear light mind has realized the emptiness of inherent existence intuitively or not. The meditator who has attained the impure illusory body, which is reached prior to the attainment of the pure illusory body, is not yet an arya being (noble one) because he or she has not yet realized emptiness intuitively with the mind of simultaneous great bliss. Anyone who has attained the meaning clear light and thus the intuitive realization of emptiness has become a secret mantra arya being, and his or her subsequent pure illusory body is far superior to the impure one.

When the meditator attains the impure illusory body, he or she has entered the third of the five stages or divisions of the completion stage. For this reason the impure illusory body is also known as the illusory body of the third stage. It is attained when the meditative equipoise of ultimate example clear light has ceased and the first mind of the reverse order—that of black near-attainment—immediately arises. At that very instant the fully accomplished meditator will achieve the impure illusory body.

There are many reasons why the meditator reaches the impure illusory body at that time. First of all, while on the generation stage that meditator had much experience in taking the intermediate state to the path of the complete enjoyment body (section 6). Furthermore he or she has extensively practised the completion stage meditations of mixing the enjoyment body during waking and sleep (sections 31 and 35). Finally, the meditator has attained the isolated mind of ultimate example clear light through the force of the yogas of the isolation of speech, such as the inner fire meditation (section 15) and the vajra recitation. It is through the accumulated experience of all these practices that the impure illusory body is attained when the isolated mind of the ultimate example clear light ceases. In general, merely understanding the illusory body intellectually is a source for accumulating much meritorious power. Secret mantra meditators look upon the illusory body as an ever-flowing fountain of encouragement to practise and as an object truly worthy of attainment.

Through the infinite kindness of Je Tsong-khapa the perfect methods by which meditators can attain a flawless realization of the illusory body have been preserved. These methods are free from even the slightest corruption and are set forth with crystal clarity. The translator Tak-tsang praised Tsong-khapa's explanation of the illusory body very highly and the Eighth Karmapa Mikyö Dorje (1507-1554) also admired his commentarial works.[17]

The outstanding qualities of the illusory body cannot be stressed too much. Nowadays some people are excited by stories of super-normal powers but in fact powers such as levitation, clairvoyance and magic are relatively easy to attain. In India, for example, there are many magicians but they are not highly respected by the society. People come to see them the same way a westerner might look at television, for entertainment. Although the audience may pay some money to see him perform his tricks, they do not think, 'May I become like that magician!' Instead of being objects of respect and admiration, such illusionists are often treated rudely by the police and others. The attainment of the illusory body however, is a completely transcendent phenomenon. Once you have achieved it, the highest and purest form of super-normal powers will come to you naturally and effortlessly. Thus it is infinitely fortunate that uncorrupted teachings on the illusory body are still available to us during these degenerate times.

In Nagarjuna's *Five Stages* there are three verses explaining the basis for achieving the illusory body. First, he states that sentient beings are born in cyclic existence not by choice but through causes and conditions, and the main cause is the mind of clear light—that is the fourth empty or the 'all empty' clear light. Second, although the all empty clear light is the cause of ordinary beings' bondage in cyclic existence, it is the cause for accomplished yogis to attain the illusory body and, as a result, perfect enlightenment. Third, Nagarjuna states that there is no experiencer of the sufferings of cyclic existence other than the 'I' that is merely imputed by thought in dependence upon the very subtle mind and its associated wind. An examination of these three statements will show how they clearly demonstrate the basis for attaining the illusory body.

The all empty clear light is said to be the cause of rebirth in cyclic existence and hence of all suffering because rebirth depends upon the preceding intermediate state existence and this in turn depends upon the all empty clear light of a previous death. This does not contradict in any way the assertion in sutra that cyclic existence is caused by conceptualizing a truly-existent self, or self-grasping. The distinguishing factor of secret mantra is its assertion that the deluded mind of self-grasping depends upon its gross mounted wind. This gross wind developed from a subtle one which in turn developed from the very subtle wind mounted by the all empty mind of clear light. This is the reason behind the first statement that the all empty clear light is the cause of rebirth for ordinary beings.

However, although the all empty clear light causes ordinary beings to be reborn in cyclic existence with a contaminated body, it causes accomplished yogis to attain the body of a deity (the illusory body) within that deity's mandala. Without using this clear light and its mounted wind there is no way for these yogis to achieve this illusory body. Therefore, their practice is to perceive this all empty clear light through the force of the yoga of the isolation of speech (e.g. through inner fire meditation). Eventually, the mind of this clear light transforms into the mind of the illusory body while its mounted wind transforms into the illusory body itself. Thus Nagarjuna's second statement is a clear indication that the very subtle wind upon which is mounted the all empty mind of clear light is the basis for attaining the illusory body.

As for the third statement concerning the 'experiencer of suffering', this indicates that while the gross body and mind are temporary bases upon which the 'I' is imputed, the *primary* and *continuously residing* bases of imputation are the very subtle mind and its mounted wind. This does not deny an imputed self that is imputed on the gross physical body and mind for, in fact, there are two types of body: the gross and the subtle. The gross body is the temporary one while the very subtle wind is the body of the continuously residing continuum.

The gross human body is temporary because it is produced from the uniting sperm and egg of one's parents and must be left behind at the time of death. The subtle body of the continuously residing continuum on the other hand, never dies. To use an analogy, the heat of hot water is temporary, but the wetness of water is never separate from the water itself. Whenever there is water (in its liquid form) there is always wetness. In the same way, the continuously residing body—the very suble wind—is never separate from the continuously residing self. You have never been separated from it in the past nor will you ever be separated from it in the future. Because this body is the very subtle wind—which is quite different from the external wind that blows upon the earth—it is in the nature of lightness and movement. The temporary gross body is like the house in which this continuously residing body is temporarily dwelling. At the time of death this subtle body leaves its temporary dwelling and moves on to another life in the same way that travellers must leave one hotel and move on to the next.

The explanation of the actual method to attain the
illusory body (75)

For the illusory body to be attained the practitioner must be
able to separate the subtle and gross bodies through the force
of meditation. There are certain times when these two bodies
separate in the life of any individual but, because this does not
happen through the force of meditation, it does not lead to the
attainment of the illusory body. Such a naturally occurring separation takes place at the time of death and also temporarily
during sleep. Accomplished yogis can separate the two while
awake through the force of completion stage meditation and
this is what is necessary. Anyone unable to cause such a
separation will be unable to have his or her subtle body arise
in the form of the personal deity.

There are two principal ways by which the gross and subtle
bodies can be separated through the force of meditation. The
first method is the transference of consciousness (Tib. po-wa)
as explained in Naropa's *Six Practices*. Here the practitioner
isolates the very subtle wind and the mind mounted upon it
and then ejects them through the crown of the head. This
method relies upon certain visualization practices and the
holding of the vase breath and is repeated again and again
until signs of accomplishment are received. This is not a very
difficult practice but it will not be explained here because,
even though it does lead to the separation of the two bodies, it
is not helpful in attaining the illusory body.

To separate the gross and subtle bodies in a manner that will
bring about the attainment of the illusory body depends upon
utilizing the eight signs—from the mirage-like vision to the
clear light—of the serial order. These signs should be experienced at their deepest and strongest level so that they appear to
you as vividly as if you were actually dying. In the past it has
happened that a meditator has experienced only the superficial
level of these signs but mistakenly thought, because unaware of
the many different levels of this experience, that he or she had
in fact attained the actual isolated mind of ultimate example
clear light. When such a meditator arises from equipoise he

mistakenly believes he has attained the actual body of his personal deity and when he re-enters the equipoise of clear light he feels he has achieved the actual union of the two truths. Afterwards, merely because his mind has become somewhat clearer than before he believes he has reached buddhahood. In actuality, however, none of these supposed accomplishments have happened at all.

Just as various grades of gold have a different value because of their varying purity, so too do the different levels of clear light experience have differing worth. To be able to attain the actual illusory body it is first necessary to achieve the actual isolated mind of ultimate example clear light, and to do this successfully requires becoming familiar with the different levels or grades of clear light experience by engaging in the appropriate meditation again and again.

Once you have attained the isolated mind of ultimate example clear light through the force of meditation, the yoga of this isolated mind will directly cause the gross and subtle bodies to separate. It is the all empty clear light of death that normally causes these two bodies to separate; therefore, if you want this separation to take place *before* death, you must be able to attain the isolated mind of ultimate example clear light yogically. This depends on attaining the isolation of speech through the yoga of inner fire or the yoga of vajra recitation. These two yogas are indirectly responsible for causing the two bodies to separate. However, inner fire practices themselves will only be able to carry you to the isolated mind of *non-ultimate* example clear light. If you want to attain the *ultimate* example clear light before death, you must depend upon an action seal (section 42). Inner fire and vajra recitation by themselves are not sufficient causes for all the pervading winds to dissolve into the indestructible drop at the heart as they do in death.

When the accomplished practitioner arises from the isolated mind of ultimate example clear light, he or she does so with the same motivation as when arising from the truth body during the practice of the mixings with the complete enjoyment body. The yogi desires to attain the illusory body for the sake of all beings and subsequently arises in the form of this body whose nature can be explained in terms of the following twelve similes. In Aryadeva's *Wisdom Vajra Compendium* it is said that the illusory body is like: (1) an illusion, (2) the reflection of the moon in water, (3) the body's shadow, (4) a mirage, (5) a dream, (6) an echo, (7) a city of intermediate state beings (literally 'smell-eaters'), (8) an hallucination, (9) a rainbow, (10) a bolt of lightning, (11) a water bubble and (12) a reflection in a mirror. These are explained as follows.

(1) An illusory person—that is someone created by a magician—appears to be endowed with limbs and so forth like a real person, but is in actuality merely a mental appearance conjured up through the force of spells and the like. Similarly, the illusory body, though endowed with limbs and so forth, is actually in the mere nature of subtle wind and the mind mounted upon it. When you reach buddhahood it is not your gross body that becomes a buddha's holy form body. Rather, when you attain the illusory body you gain a new body that is different from the gross one and it is this new body that will transform into a buddha's form body. Thus it is said that the illusory body is like an illusion.

(2) There are countless bodies of water upon the earth and on a clear night each one will bear a reflection of the moon. Although there are many reflections, they are all of the same moon. Similarly, a yogi who has attained the illusory body can emanate thousands of different forms according to the needs of sentient beings. Though in actuality there is only one yogi, his emanations reach countless beings. Furthermore, just as the reflection of the moon appears in many bodies of water at the same time, so can the yogi manifest in many forms simultaneously. Thus it is said that the illusory body is like the reflection of the moon· in water.

(3) The body's shadow has a head, arms, legs and a trunk, and so does the illusory body. The shadow is empty of substantiality and contains no inner organs and the same is true of

the illusory body. Inside the shadow there are no hollow spaces and neither are there any within the illusory body. Finally, the shadow is not produced by the meeting of the sperm and egg of the parents and neither is the illusory body. Thus it is said that the illusory body is like the body's shadow.

(4) The illusory body is said to be like an indestructible vajra because it is free from death. However, this does not mean that the illusory body is a permanent phenomenon; it is impermanent because it undergoes change from moment to moment. This quality of impermanence is demonstrated by the example of a shimmering mirage which also changes from moment to moment. Thus it is said that the illusory body is like a mirage.

(5) The dream body is the best example for the illusory body because their natures, substances and causes are very similar. Furthermore, the dream body can actually be mixed with the illusory body while practising the mixing with the enjoyment body during sleep (section 35). The dream body is the only one that can be mixed in this way with the illusory body and therefore provides the best illustration of the existence of the illusory body. The major difference between these two bodies is in terms of their qualities; the illusory body has many excellent attributes not shared by the dream body. Otherwise they are very similar.

If you understand how the dream body is formed, how it differs from the gross physical body, how it dissolves into the physical body when you wake from the dream and how it remains with you in an unmanifest state while awake, you can understand the same four things about the illusory body. The dream body and the illusory body both arise from the all empty clear light instantaneously with the appearance of the mind of black near-attainment of the reverse order. They are also of the same substance, namely the very subtle wind. Knowing about the dream body, therefore, gives insight into the nature, substance and means of attaining the illusory body. Thus it is said that the illusory body is like a dream.

(6) A yogi who has attained the illusory body may, for the

sake of an example, manifest as a tiger and as a dog at the same time. The forms of these animals appear to the yogi as different entities from one another and from his own form; in reality, however, they both arose from the yogi himself. Although they are manifestations, they seem to exist as things external to the yogi. This is similar to someone's experience with an echo. When he hears an echo, it seems as if the sound is coming from the outside, while in truth it was he himself who produced the sound in the first place. Thus it is said that the illusory body is like an echo.

(7) To intermediate state beings—called smell-eaters because they are sustained by odours—the cities they inhabit seem to arise instantly and all at once and when they cease they seem to disappear in the same instantaneous fashion. Similarly, a yogi who has achieved the illusory body feels that his or her mandala with its associated deities arises suddenly and when it ceases it seems to disappear suddenly as well. Thus it is said that the illusory body is like a city of smell-eaters.

(8) A person may have the miraculous power to manifest a large number of tigers at once. Even though he sees these tigers, they are in reality nothing but himself. (When ordinary people see these emanated tigers, they are hallucinating. Thus this appearance is called a visual hallucination.) In a similar fashion, when a yogi who has reached the illusory body sends out emanations, all these apparently numerous beings are in fact just the yogi himself. Thus it is said that the illusory body is like an hallucination.

(9) Just as the colours of a rainbow are unmixed and the rainbow possesses no quality of obstructing contact, the same is true of the illusory body. Thus it is said that the illusory body is like a rainbow.

(10) Just as lightning springs from the midst of clouds, the illusory body arises from the old gross body. Thus it is said that the illusory body is like a bolt of lightning.

(11) Just as a water bubble arises instantly from water itself and is the nature of water, so too does the illusory body arise instantly from the state of emptiness and is in the nature of

emptiness. Thus it is said that the illusory body is like a water bubble.

(12) When a person stands before a mirror, all the parts of the reflection—the body, limbs and so forth—develop instantly and are very clear and lucid. In the same way, the illusory body and all its parts develop instantly and are of a clear and transparent nature. Thus it is said that the illusory body is like a reflection in a mirror.

In the sutra teachings, these twelve examples are used to demonstrate the way in which all phenomena lack inherent existence. Here they are used to explain the illusory body.

There are many synonyms to refer to this body and the ones listed below come from the *Guhyasamaja Tantra*. A brief explanation of each will help to provide an understanding of the excellent qualities of such a body.

When the illusory body is referred to as the 'blessing of the self' this 'self' should be understood as that which is imputed on the very subtle wind and mind. 'Blessing' refers to the transformation of these bases of imputation into the illusory body's body and mind. As for the term 'illusory body' itself, this indicates that it is a body which is like an illusion, as explained in the list of twelve similes. The illusory body is also known as the 'deceptive truth' because it itself is conventional, or deceptive, and not ultimate.

Three additional terms for the illusory body are the 'complete enjoyment body', 'Vajrasattva' (the vajra-being) and 'Vajradhara' (the vajra-holder). However, the use of these terms does not mean that the illusory body itself is the actual *resultant* enjoyment body, Vajrasattva or Vajradhara. Rather, it is the *path* enjoyment body, etc. Finally, when the illusory body is called the 'vajra body' this means that the impure illusory body is *like* the vajra body while the pure illusory body is the actual vajra body itself.

As for the benefits of attaining the illusory body, these are also enumerated in the *Guhyasamaja Tantra* as well as in the *Five Stages* and *Condensed Deeds*. Thus it is said that the illusory body: is adorned with the thirty-two noble symbols and the eighty noble examples, is the object of offering for all human and celestial beings, can obtain wealth and possessions effortlessly, is free from poverty, sickness, old age, death, rebirth and all the sufferings of cyclic existence and can manifest various forms to benefit others. Most importantly, it is definite that the possessor of the illusory body will attain buddhahood within that very lifetime.

9 Clear Light and Union

The explanation of the stages for attaining the ultimate clear light (76)
   This has three divisions:

   77 The method of manifesting the ultimate clear light
   78 How the ultimate clear light is actually accomplished through this method
   79 Why the ultimate clear light destroys both intellectually acquired and innate delusions simultaneously

The method of manifesting the ultimate clear light (77)
   It is said that the realizations of a secret mantra meditator who has reached the generation stage are almost equal to those of a sutra meditator who has achieved the eighth level of an arya bodhisattva, while the realizations of one who has reached the impure illusory body are almost equal to those of an arya of the tenth level of sutra. In the sutra system, the state of an arya is reached when emptiness is realized intuitively with the gross level of consciousness, but this is not sufficient for becoming a secret mantra arya. Until a meditator has been able to realize emptiness intuitively *with the mind of simultaneous great bliss* he or she has still not attained the spiritual

path of an arya being according to secret mantra. Thus once you have attained the impure illusory body it is necessary to achieve the realization of the meaning clear light whereby emptiness is cognized directly and intuitively—without reliance upon a mental image—by the subtlest of minds. This is what is meant by manifesting the ultimate clear light.

The practice of penetrating the vital points of one's own body through meditating on the channels, winds and drops— as in the yogas of inner fire and vajra recitation—does not have the power to carry you to the attainment of the meaning clear light. Thus such meditations are said to be completed for anyone who has reached the impure illusory body. Now it is necessary to follow either the external or internal approach to the attainment of the meaning clear light. Two practices make up the internal method and these are the concentrations known as 'subsequent destruction' and 'holding the body entirely'. The external method is the yoga of depending on an action seal. These three will now be explained briefly.

To reach the concentration known as subsequent destruction first visualize that the entire vessel-like phenomenal universe and all the sentient beings contained therein melt into light which then dissolves into you. Then you yourself dissolve from the bottom and top simultaneously, like a candle burning from both ends. Gradually your entire body will dissolve into the indestructible drop at your heart. With this dissolution the very subtle mind of clear light will arise and you should hold onto it with single-pointed concentration. The technical method by which it is carried out is as follows.

You begin by visualizing the impure illusory body as a wisdom being—the white form of your personal deity—residing in the heart of your old aggregate of form. If, for example, your personal deity is Heruka, the illusory body is visualised as a white Heruka in the heart of your old aggregate of form, which itself is visualized as the blue commitment being Heruka. (The same is true for the practice of Guhyasamaja or of Yamantaka; however, if your personal deity is Vajrayogini, the commitment being should be seen in red colour.)

As the commitment being Heruka you now have the white illusory body Heruka in your heart. From the heart of this illusory body infinite rays of brilliant blue light shine forth and pervade the vast phenomenal universe and all the sentient beings therein. This light purifies all negativities—no matter how subtle—and causes all places and beings to melt into light which then dissolves back into the heart of the illusory body Heruka. Next the blue commitment being Heruka begins to melt simultaneously from its crown and feet and eventually so does the white wisdom being. Finally, nothing is left but the indestructible drop.

Once the impure illusory body has been attained it will be very easy to dissolve all the winds into the indestructible drop through the force of such meditation because the yogas of the isolation of speech have already been successfully completed and your winds are now very supple and easily controlled. As a result of this dissolution you will experience all eight signs—from the mirage to the clear light—as vividly as if you were actually dying. As these eight signs arise they are experienced in conjunction with emptiness. Finally, with the arisal of the all empty clear light you should meditate single-pointedly upon emptiness for a prolonged period of time. By doing such a meditation again and again this all empty clear light will eventually realize emptiness intuitively and you will thereby attain the meaning clear light.

The other internal method is the concentration known as holding the body entirely, meaning that the entire body melts into light, dissolves into emptiness and that emptiness is held by concentration. In this practice the commitment being simply melts simultaneously from the crown and the feet into the indestructible drop without first sending out light from the illusory body and dissolving the universe and its contents. As the light of the dissolving body melts into the indestructible drop the all empty clear light will arise and, as before, you should use this very subtle mind to meditate single-pointedly on emptiness. Again, after repeated practice this will lead to the attainment of the meaning clear light. On the generation stage these two internal concentrations of subsequent destruction and holding the body entirely are also performed but their power is less because the meditator's level of realization is less.

In the external method it is the yoga of the action seal that causes all the winds to dissolve into the indestructible drop with the result that the eight signs appear as vividly as in death. As before, these signs should be experienced in conjunction with emptiness meditation so that when the all empty clear light arises you can concentrate single-pointedly upon emptiness with that very subtle mind for a long time. A yogi who can derive the clear light in dependence upon an action seal will experience inexhaustible simultaneous great bliss and other inner realizations. It is for this reason that Long-döl Lama said that the action seal is like a wish-fulfulling cow from which you receive an inexhaustible supply of milk. However, this does not apply to everyone; it is only true for a qualified, accomplished meditator.

How the ultimate clear light is actually accomplished through this method (78)

In the tantric texts it says that the meditator will achieve the meaning clear light at dawn just as all beings who are going to reach enlightenment will do so at dawn. For example, Shakyamuni Buddha, after sitting beneath the tree of enlightenment in Bodh Gaya, demonstrated destroying all maras (demonic interferences) in the evening, entering meditative equipoise at midnight and attaining full enlightenment at dawn.

When the practitioner who has attained the impure illusory body meditates again and again in accordance with the methods explained above, eventually he or she will receive dreams and visions that indicate the attainment of the meaning clear light is near. When these special signs appear the meditator makes elaborate offerings to the spiritual master and tries to please him. Then at midnight the disciple will receive the third empowerment—the knowledge-wisdom empowerment—directly from the master. The meditator had in fact received this empowerment before but because he or she lacked pure understanding the action seal given at that time was only a visualized one. Now that the meditator is about to achieve the meaning clear light, however, he or she is qualified to receive an actual action seal and the actual knowledge-wisdom empowerment.

When the yogi embraces the action seal he or she will experience the eight signs as vividly as in death. As explained before, these signs are experienced in conjunction with emptiness and when the all empty clear light realizes emptiness intuitively the meditator will simultaneously attain the meaning clear light.

Because the isolated mind of ultimate example clear light still had a very subtle dualistic appearance it was not able to realize emptiness intuitively. With the attainment of the meaning clear light at dawn this subtle conceptual realization of emptiness will be transformed into a direct, intuitive realization and the meditator will thereby attain the spiritual path of the secret mantra arya: the secret mantra path of seeing. With the attainment of the meaning clear light the impure illusory body will disappear like a rainbow in the sky. Because it ceases in this way the impure illusory body is said to be *like* the vajra body but is not the actual vajra body itself. When the meditator arises from the meditative equipoise in which the meaning clear light is first attained, he arises in a new form, the pure illusory body.

Why the ultimate clear light destroys both intellectually acquired and innate delusions simultaneously (79)

According to the perfection vehicle of sutra, when you have attained the path of seeing by gaining an intuitive realization of emptiness (with the gross mind) you become an arya bodhisattva of the first level or ground. While remaining on the path of seeing you abandon the intellectually acquired delusions and it is only when you reach the eighth ground of the path of meditation that you have abandoned the innate delusions as well. According to secret mantra, however, the yogi who has attained the meaning clear light is able to abandon both types of delusion at the same time by means of one path. Why is this possible?

Anyone who has attained the meaning clear light has previously meditated extensively upon the isolated mind of ultimate example clear light and the impure illusory body and thus has accumulated a vast store of wisdom and merit. (As stated, wisdom is accumulated through the force of the isolated mind of ultimate example clear light and merit through the force of the illusory body.) Therefore, the meaning clear light has tremendous strength because it is empowered by this vast dual accumulation. It is this superior strength that enables the meaning clear light to destroy both kinds of delusions simultaneously within a single meditation session. This ability is unique to the practices of highest yoga tantra.

When the yogi emerges from the state of meaning clear light the mind of black near-attainment of the reverse order will arise. At that time the pure illusory body is attained as well as the secret mantra path of meditation. With the abandonment of intellectually acquired and innate obscurations preventing liberation the yogi has become a secret mantra arhat, or foe destroyer.

The meaning clear light is known by many names. Along with the example clear light it is known as the definitive meaning of Heruka, the interpretative meaning being the Heruka who is blue in colour, embraces his consort and so forth. The meaning clear light is also known as the inner sky-enjoyer. Of the two types of sky-enjoyer, the outer—the pure land of Vajrayogini—is achieved through reliance upon the generation stage and the inner through reliance upon the completion stage. The terms 'meaning clear light', 'clear light of the fourth stage' and 'inner sky-enjoyer' are all synonymous. The meaning clear light is called the inner sky-enjoyer because it enjoys or has the freedom to use the sky, which refers to emptiness, intuitively.

The yogi who has attained the inner sky-enjoyer has also attained the outer one. Through the force of purifying his or her mind inwardly, the external environment is also purified.

Once the mind is free from all impurities there are no further impure external appearances left. This is true according to both sutra and secret mantra. Thus the yogi who has attained the meaning clear light has gone to the pure land of Vajrayogini. Such a pure land is not a long distance away in miles; it can be reached by following the completion stage practices. But as long as your mind is tainted by impurities you would not be able to perceive this pure land even if you were living in the centre of it. Therefore, to reach such a pure land it is very important to practise the isolated body whereby ordinary appearances are prevented from arising.

The actual explanation of the mahamudra that is the union of the two truths (80)

This is divided into:

81 The introduction to the union
82 An explanation of when the union is attained

The introduction to the union (81)

The mahamudra that is the union of the two truths is also known as the union needing practice. The union not needing practice is attained at the first moment of the path of no more learning, which is simultaneous with the attainment of perfect buddhahood.

As mentioned before, the union needing practice is the fifth of the five stages or divisions of the completion stage. It depends upon the fourth stage which is attained at the moment the meaning clear light is experienced. This in turn depends upon the third stage which is attained at the first moment of the impure illusory body. This depends on the second: the first moment of the isolation of mind. And this depends upon the first stage: the yoga of the isolation of speech, which in turn depends upon having practised the isolation of body. Thus all five stages are related to one another by the chain of cause and effect. It is important to understand the precise meaning of each of these five stages and not be misled by their titles.

The term 'union' can refer to many different things: the union of the two truths, the union of simultaneous great bliss and emptiness, the union of body and mind and so forth. Here it refers to the union of the two truths but these should not be understood in the same way as the two truths of sutra, although they have the same names. According to the maha-mudra of secret mantra it is the pure illusory body that is the deceptive truth and the meaning clear light that is the ultimate truth. In general, according to sutra, any phenomenon other than emptiness itself is a deceptive, or conventional, truth. Because meditation upon the illusory body emphasizes such deceptive truths the illusory body itself is known by this name. In a similar fashion, because meditation upon the mean-ing clear light emphasizes emptiness, it itself is called ultimate truth. However, the meaning clear light is not actually an ulti-mate truth; because it is a mind it must necessarily be a deceptive truth. It is the *object* of this mind that is the ultimate truth.

The Sanskrit word for union is yuganaddha: yuga signifying 'two' and naddha signifying 'simultaneously assembled' or 'non-dual'. Thus this term refers to the union of meaning clear light and the pure illusory body and the fact that these two elements are gathered together simultaneously within the continuum of a single person. An ordinary being simul-taneously possesses a body and a mind and together they form the basis upon which the person is imputed. In the case of a yogi who has attained the fifth stage, his or her body is the pure illusory body while the mind is the meaning clear light; these two together are the basis upon which the person of that yogi is imputed.

An explanation of when this union is attained (82)

Some texts state that this union is attained when the mind of white appearance of the reverse order ceases. This is incorrect. The pure illusory body develops from the very subtle wind upon which the mind of initial meaning clear light is mounted and is attained automatically and without effort the instant this mind ceases. Thus, the pure illusory body is attained at the first instant of the mind of black near-attainment of the reverse order.

The illusory body is a new body and when the yogi initially achieves it he or she no longer has the mind of meaning clear light. As stated, that mind has already ceased to exist the instant the mind of black near-attainment of the reverse order arose. Within that same meditation session the yogi perceives the remaining reverse order signs, up to and including the mirage. Then he or she engages in the activities of the post meditation, or subsequent realization, session while still possessing the pure illusory body, which is unceasing.

Afterwards, by depending upon one of the internal or external methods mentioned earlier, the yogi will experience all the serial order signs from the mirage up to and including the all empty clear light. These signs are experienced in conjunction with meditation upon emptiness and when the all empty sign is perceived this is again the meaning clear light. When this is attained the yogi simultaneously reaches the mahamudra that is the union of the two truths. That yogi has assembled the pure illusory body and the meaning clear light at the same time. Even though the union needing practice has now been attained, the yogi will again arise from the meaning clear light. Thus in order to attain buddhahood there are further practices to be performed.

The body of a meditator who has attained the meaning clear light is known as the union body. When you have attained the pure illusory body you can manifest in two ways. First, you can emanate various beneficial aspects to suit the specific needs of sentient beings. Second, by having the pure illusory body in the form of the wisdom being enter into your old aggregate of form, you can show this gross body to others and with it engage in such beneficial activities as expounding the dharma and so forth. In the latter case the gross body is like a house and the pure illusory body is like a person living within it. To use another analogy, the pure illusory body is like a pre-

cious jewel and the old aggregate of form is like the treasure
chest in which it is kept.

Although everyone can see the container—the gross body—
very few people know that there is a precious treasure within.
When Nagarjuna reached the union body within his lifetime
he would go from place to place teaching the dharma to his
numerous disciples. When ordinary beings saw him they
perceived nothing but a simple monk; they did not realize that
within his heart his pure illusory body resided in the form of a
wisdom being. Many other spiritual masters also attained the
union body within their lifetimes. Gyalwa Ensapa and the
great yogi Dharma Vajra are just two of the many who could
be mentioned. One of the most famous of all was Milarepa
who, although his attainment of the union body freed him
from all poverty, would still go from village to village seeking
food. His physical body was so emaciated that people would
take pity on him thinking him to be a poor beggar. When he
passed away and his body was cremated, however, many
miraculous signs appeared attesting to his great spiritual
advancement. Yet even these signs were not seen by everyone
in the same way: different people saw different things in accordance with their own level of spiritual development. If
Milarepa were to be judged merely from an external point of
view it would be very difficult to understand that he was, in
fact, a fully enlightened buddha.

The old aggregate of form of someone who has attained the
illusory body does not appear to others as any different from
the way it looked before the illusory body was achieved. For
example, if someone you had known for many years were to
attain the union body, unless you yourself had also attained
the illusory body you would not be able to detect any
difference in your friend's appearance. In truth, however,
your friend's actual body is now the pure illusory body and his
or her actual mind is the meaning clear light. It is only to help
others unable to perceive his or her actual form that the
meditator keeps and displays the old gross form.

In the profound rite known as the *Offering to the Spiritual*

Master the spiritual master is visualized in the external form of a monk. In his heart is the Buddha Vajradhara and in Vajradhara's heart is the letter *huṁ*. This visualization represents the three secret mantra beings: the external form is the commitment being, Vajradhara is the wisdom being and the *huṁ* is the concentration being. Furthermore, the commitment being is the spiritual master's physical body, the wisdom being is his pure illusory body—his actual body—and the concentration being is his actual mind—the meaning clear light. Once the existence of this union body is understood, it is not difficult to recognize your spiritual master as being an actual buddha.

10　The Resultant Mahamudra

The resultant mahamudra union which has the seven features of the father and mother facing one another (83)

The explanation of the causal mahamudra meditations has now been completed including the instructions on the union needing practice. The goal of all mahayana training is the attainment of full enlightenment: the union not needing practice. This is the resultant mahamudra and is presented in five divisions:

84　The explanation of the places where buddhahood can be attained

85　The explanation of the three kinds of being who can attain buddhahood

86　The explanation of the ways in which buddhahood is attained by the three kinds of being

90　The excellent qualities of buddhahood

91　The relationship between the stages of the path in sequential and reverse order

The explanation of the places where buddhahood can be attained (84)

According to secret mantra there are three places in which

buddhahood can be achieved: (1) in the field of Akanishta, (2) in the desire realm and (3) in a place that is neither Akanishta nor the desire realm. In the mahayana sutras, however, it is asserted that there is only one place in which a being can reach perfect buddhahood and that place is Akanishta. Considering that it was Shakyamuni Buddha who made both assertions, which one is to be accepted as correct? Isn't there a contradiction here between sutra and secret mantra? In actuality there is no contradiction. Buddha's assertion that full enlightenment can only be attained in Akanishta was made with specific disciples in mind: those who do not have a strong mind or lack the ability to practise the highest form of secret mantra. To those who are able to practise highest yoga tantra, however, Buddha taught that enlightenment could be attained while still in the desire realm. Thus there is actually no discrepancy between these two assertions; it is only because they are meant for beings of different capacities that there appears to be a contradiction between them.

In this case Buddha's secret mantra teachings convey his ultimate intention in the same way that the Middle Way Consequentialist system conveys his ultimate philosophical intention. Buddha taught four different philosophical systems in accordance with the different capacities of his disciples and each system claims to be the correct path leading to a realization of emptiness. These four systems appear to contradict one another but in fact they provide a graded sequence of training whereby the correct view of emptiness can eventually be attained. The only way to prove that the Middle Way Consequentialist system is the only ultimately correct system is through logical reasoning and personal experience. In a similar fashion, secret mantra is proved to be the ultimate method by the fact that those who have the ability to practise highest yoga tantra can attain perfect buddhahood within a single lifetime. In fact, it is only through highest yoga tantra that a practitioner can reach perfect buddhahood at all.

According to secret mantra, buddhahood is attained in Akanishta by a very special type of practitioner. This is the bodhisattva who has reached the tenth ground through the sutra paths of the perfection vehicle. Such a bodhisattva will not be able to proceed past this tenth ground without engaging in the practices of highest yoga tantra. Therefore, until he receives the empowerments of secret mantra and enters into the actual paths of highest yoga tantra, it will be impossible for him to attain buddhahood. Such a bodhisattva receives these empowerments and then achieves enlightenment in Akanishta.

If the practitioner is someone who has followed the two stages of secret mantra gradually from the beginning and is going to achieve enlightenment in that lifetime, then it is definite that he or she will attain buddhahood within the desire realm. For example, the three yogis mentioned earlier— Gyalwa Ensapa, Dharma Vajra and Milarepa—all reached buddhahood in Tibet.

Finally, the third place in which buddhahood can be attained is neither Akanishta nor the desire realm. Buddhahood is attained here by a secret mantra practitioner who attains the isolated mind of ultimate example clear light at the time of death. When the clear light of death ceases such a practitioner will achieve the illusory body instead of taking the ordinary intermediate state body. It is with this illusory body—in a place that is neither Akanishta nor the desire realm—that such a bodhisattva attains buddhahood.

The explanation of the three kinds of being who can attain buddhahood (85)

These three kinds of being have already been mentioned in the preceding section. To repeat, those who attain buddhahood in Akanishta are the bodhisattvas of the tenth ground of the perfection vehicle; those who attain it in the desire realm are human beings who have accomplished the five stages of the completion stage and those who attain it in the place that is neither are those who achieve the illusory body instead of the intermediate state after the clear light of death has ceased. There are no other types of being who can attain buddhahood and no other places in which such enlightenment can be reached.

There are three realms within cyclic existence: the desire realm, the form realm and the formless realm. Of all the beings in the desire realm only humans can attain buddhahood within one lifetime because only they are endowed with the physical prerequisites listed earlier (section 11). Among the form realm beings only the tenth level bodhisattvas dwelling in Akanishta can reach enlightenment via the path of secret mantra. As for the formless realm beings, none of them can progress towards enlightenment through the paths of either sutra or secret mantra.

The explanation of the ways in which buddhahood is attained by the three kinds of being (86)

This explanation is given in three parts, each one corresponding to one of the three beings described above, as follows:

87 How buddhahood is attained in Akanishta
88 How buddhahood is attained in the desire realm
89 How buddhahood is attained in the place that is neither

How buddhahood is attained in Akanishta (87)

Earlier in the text it was stated that in order to practise highest yoga tantra from the beginning a person must have the six elements found within the human body. The tenth ground bodhisattva in Akanishta, however, is a special case. His body is that of a form realm god, but because it contains the red and white drops he can experience the simultaneous great bliss that arises in dependence upon these elements. Thus he is not an ordinary god of the form realm.

When such a bodhisattva is abiding on the tenth ground the buddhas of the ten directions gather around him and encourage him to enter the path of secret mantra. They point out that his present meditative concentration is not powerful enough to annihilate the obscurations preventing omniscience and bring him to enlightenment; only the meaning clear light has such power. They will then confer on him the knowledge-wisdom empowerment and present him with an action seal. The bodhisattva then enters into meditation with his consort and experiences the eight signs from the mirage to the all empty clear light in conjunction with emptiness. When the all empty clear light of simultaneous great bliss realizes emptiness intuitively the bodhisattva attains the meaning clear light. Thus he is an exception in that he does not need to practise the generation stage or any meditation up to and including the impure illusory body of the completion stage in order to reach the meaning clear light.

With the attainment of the meaning clear light the bodhisattva enters the spiritual path of a secret mantra arya—the secret mantra path of seeing—and the fourth stage of the completion stage. Following this, at the first instant of the mind of black near-attainment of the reverse order, he will attain the pure illusory body—the union body—and enter the secret mantra path of meditation. Then, the next time he enters the meditative equipoise of meaning clear light he will attain the union heart and the fifth stage of the completion stage: the union needing practice. Finally, he will enter into the meditative equipoise in which the very last obscurations preventing omniscience are removed. At that point he has achieved the path of no more learning, full omniscience and the resultant mahamudra union having the seven features: perfect buddhahood itself.

This way of achieving buddhahood is peculiar to the tenth ground bodhisattva of the perfection vehicle. He is able to attain enlightenment in this way through the force of the vast accumulations of merit and wisdom already collected during countless aeons on the sutra path.

How buddhahood is attained in the desire realm (88)

Most practitioners of the path of secret mantra will attain buddhahood through the form of a desire realm human. As explained before, a yogi who has reached the fifth stage—the union needing practice—has nearly completed the entire path. There remains no new object of knowledge to be realized; all that is necessary is to improve the quality of what has already been experienced. It is by doing this that the remaining obstacles to enlightenment—the obscurations preventing omniscience—are removed and buddhahood is achieved.

These obscurations or coverings are what keep the mind from realizing all objects of knowledge simultaneously. Even though a yogi of the fifth stage is very advanced, he or she still possesses these hindrances. When such a yogi is in the state of meditative equipoise on emptiness, he or she cannot at the same time perform such actions as giving teachings. In other words, the yogi cannot be absorbed in meditative equipoise and engage in the activities of subsequent realization simultaneously but can only be in either one state or the other. A fully realized buddha, on the other hand, has the ability to perform beneficial deeds without ever arising from deep meditation upon the ultimate nature of reality; this is one of the excellent qualities of an enlightened being. To attain such an exalted state the yogi must repeatedly enter the meditative equipoise of meaning clear light and thereby remove all the remaining obscurations preventing omniscience. That is why the union of the fifth stage is known as the union needing practice.

The principal meditation for such a practitioner is the external method of action seal yoga together with the two internal concentrations previously described. The purpose of these practices is to eradicate all obscurations by means of the meaning clear light. The method of embracing the action seal can be explained as follows by taking the example of a man whose personal deity is Heruka. He visualizes himself as Heruka embracing his consort Vajravarahi and through the force of this embrace all his winds enter, abide and dissolve within the indestructible drop at his heart. With this dissolution the eight signs appear and are experienced in conjunction with emptiness. With arisal of the all empty clear light his mind will mingle indistinguishably with emptiness, like water being poured into water. At this stage the experienced yogi can remain in the state of all empty clear light for as long as he wishes. Until perfect buddhahood is attained this practice must be performed frequently.

When the yogi arises from the equipoise of clear light he will experience the minds of black near-attainment, red increase, white appearance and so forth. With each successive sign his mind will become more and more gross in nature until eventually he again engages in daily activities, such as expounding the dharma and so forth. During this subsequent realization stage he will no longer have the mind of clear light because it already ceased with the arisal of the mind of black near-attainment. Whenever he wishes to manifest this very subtle mind of clear light again he must either enter into meditation with the action seal or perform the internal concentrations.

The clear light experienced by someone on the level of union is the meaning clear light. By using it to meditate single-pointedly on emptiness all nine levels of the obscurations preventing omniscience will gradually be eliminated. Eventually the yogi will attain enlightenment. As was the case with the meaning clear light, this enlightenment will be achieved at dawn, the symbol of the all empty clear light.

Let us say that your personal deity is Heruka and, after accomplishing all the stages so far described, you have today received signs indicating you are ready to receive buddhahood. You then go to your spiritual master and make elaborate outer, inner and secret offerings. At midnight your spiritual master will appear to you in the form of Heruka as will all the buddhas of the ten directions of space. He then grants you the knowledge-wisdom empowerment and presents you with an action seal in the form of Vajravarahi. Through the force of embracing her you experience the eight signs and with the arisal of the all empty clear light your mind mixes indistinguishably with emptiness. You then remain in this state of equipoise until dawn.

During this time your mind of meaning clear light becomes

the direct antidote to the remaining obscurations. This antidote-like consciousness is your last mind as a sentient being (i.e. a limited being) and is known as the vajra-like concentration of the path of meditation. When this mind of vajra-like concentration overcomes the very last obscurations preventing omniscience at dawn you become a fully awakened buddha. At that time your mind of clear light realizing emptiness becomes indestructible and constant; never again will you experience the minds of black near-attainment, red increase or any of the other grosser states of consciousness. From that time onwards you experience the all empty clear light realizing emptiness without a single break in continuity.

With the total annihilation at dawn of the obscurations preventing omniscience, your mind of meaning clear light will become the resultant truth body of a buddha and your pure illusory body will become the resultant form body. You have attained the union of no more learning and of the seven features. There is no longer any difference for you between meditative equipoise and subsequent realization; all objects of knowledge will be simultaneously realized within a single mind in a single moment because even the most subtle dualistic appearance has been totally eliminated. Your clear light mind will simultaneously perceive all objects of knowledge as clearly as ordinary beings see their reflection in a mirror.

How buddhahood is attained in the place that is neither (89)

In the discussion of the four joys (section 27) it was stated that there comes a time when the secret mantra meditator who is prepared to experience the ultimate example clear light must either (1) accept an action seal and perform those practices that will cause the dissolution of the pervading wind (in addition to the other winds) into the indestructible drop at the heart or (2) decide not to accept such a seal and instead wait until the clear light of death when all the winds will naturally dissolve there. What happens in the former case has already been described; the latter case can now be explained as follows.

When the qualified yogi experiences the clear light of death he or she will attain the isolated mind of ultimate example clear light. Then, instead of entering the intermediate state when this clear light mind ceases, such a yogi will arise in the form of the illusory body in a place that is neither Akanishta nor the desire realm. If the meditator's personal deity is Heruka, then buddhahood will be achieved in Heruka's pure land; if it is Guhyasamaja, then it will be in Guhyasamaja's pure land and so forth.

The illusory body attained by this yogi is the impure illusory body because it arises through the force of the isolated mind of ultimate *example* clear light. With this impure illusory body the yogi repeatedly engages in the external method and two internal concentrations previously described, thereby experiencing the eight signs and so forth. Through these methods the meaning clear light is eventually achieved and the meditator enters the secret mantra path of seeing and becomes a secret mantra arya. Arising from this meaning clear light he or she achieves the pure illusory body and, soon afterwards, the union needing practice. From this point up until the attainment of enlightenment the path is the same as outlined before.

The excellent qualities of buddhahood (90)

The yogi who attains enlightenment does so in the form of the complete enjoyment body. Such a holy body is known as the Primordial Buddha and possesses the seven features, the second of which accounts for the name given to this union not needing practice: the resultant mahamudra union which has the seven features of the father and mother facing one another. These seven can be briefly explained as follows.

First, the complete enjoyment body is adorned by the thirty-two noble symbols and eighty noble examples. These symbols and examples are the distinctive characteristics of a buddha's form indicating the many ways in which an enlightened being is superior to ordinary sentient beings. Such characteristics include the crown protruberance (ushnisha), wisdom hair curl, elongated ears, and other marks that symbolize and exemplify the unsurpassable qualities of a fully awakened buddha. They not only indicate that a buddha is free from all the fears and sufferings of cyclic existence and has completely annihilated the obscurations preventing liberation and omniscience, but also that the enlightened being's body is not subject to degeneration, sickness, ageing or death.

Second, the complete enjoyment body is embracing his or her wisdom seal. This feature of the mother and father facing one another symbolizes that enlightenment has been achieved through completing the practices of embracing and thereby experiencing simultaneous great bliss which meditates upon emptiness.

Third, an enlightened being's mind always remains in a state of simultaneous great bliss. This is a further mark of the superiority of such a mind over the minds of mundane sentient beings.

Fourth, a buddha's simultaneous great bliss is always mixed with emptiness. Without moving from this state of total absorption an enlightened being sees all objects of knowledge as clearly as a glass bead held in one's hand. This demonstrates the exalted quality of a buddha's wisdom.

Fifth, a buddha's mind of great compassion for all sentient beings never wavers. This feature demonstrates that an enlightened being's mind is unstained by even the slightest self-cherishing thought and indicates that such a being benefits others without exception.

Sixth, the continuum of the enlightened being's body never ceases. This indicates that the indestructible vajra body has been attained.

Seventh and last, a buddha's emanations pervade the entire universe and such an enlightened being's activities for the benefit of others never cease.

This has been just a short description of the Primordial Buddha: the sambhogakaya Vajradhara. If all the excellent qualities of such a being were listed in detail, the description would run to many pages. Therefore, those wishing further explanation of the excellent qualities of a buddha's body, speech and mind should consult the eighth chapter of Maitreya's *Ornament of Clear Realizations* and its many commentaries.

The relationship between the stages of the path in sequential and reverse order (91)

By following the spiritual master you have the precious opportunity of progressing through the stages of mahayana practice and attaining the realizations of renunciation, loving kindness and the altruistic mind of enlightenment (bodhicitta) and the correct view of emptiness. With this firm foundation you are suitably qualified to enter into the practices of the generation stage meditation of secret mantra. In dependence upon the experience of the generation stage you have the opportunity to practise the isolations of body and speech of the completion stage. Through the force of accomplishing these two you can complete the practice of the isolation of mind successfully. Success in this enables you to achieve the meaning clear light. Through the force of the meaning clear light you can attain the mahamudra that is the union of the two truths. On the basis of this mahamudra you eventually attain buddhahood: the resultant mahamudra union having the seven features. This step-by-step progression from your initial dependence upon the spiritual master up to your realization of full enlightenment constitutes the sequential order relationship of the stages of the path.

As for the reverse order relationship, this is as follows. The attainment of mahamudra union having seven features depends upon your prior attainment of the mahamudra that is the union of the two truths. This in turn depends upon your attaining the meaning clear light, which depends upon the prior attainment of the illusory body. The illusory body is achieved in dependence upon attaining the isolation of mind and this in turn depends upon the isolations of speech and body of the completion stage. The realization of the isolation of body of the completion stage depends upon accomplishing the generation stage meditations and this depends upon your realization of the three principal aspects of the path: renunciation, bodhicitta and the correct view of emptiness. All the accomplishments from the attainment of buddhahood down to the development of renunciation depend upon following your spiritual master. In such a manner, then, is the reverse order relationship of the stages of the path outlined.

These two ways of looking at the interdepedent relationship between the stages of the path illustrate that if you have a sincere desire to become a buddha you must follow the *entire* path of sutra and secret mantra. Spending your life on one or two meditations will not lead you to enlightenment. If you want to have a good cup of tea it is not sufficient merely to have just the water, or just the tea, or just the milk, or just the sugar; you need to have all the ingredients together. If several different things have to be assembled merely for you to enjoy a cup of tea, how much more necessary this must be if your goal is to experience the highest enlightenment. It is unrealistic to think you can rely on just one or two isolated practices.

This completes the instructions concerning the resultant mahamudra union as well as those of the practice of secret mantra mahamudra in general. If these instructions are to be truly beneficial they should not remain the object of mere intellectual interest or curiosity: you must actually practise them under the guidance of a fully qualified spiritual master.

The concluding stages (92)

In the Kadampa tradition's teachings on the training of the mind it is stated that there are certain specific activities to be done at the beginning and the end of any dharma endeavour. No matter what action you may be engaged in—whether it be study, meditation, the practice of generosity or anything else —it is important at its outset to set a correct motivation and at its conclusion to perform a correct dedication. Setting the correct motivation was discussed at the beginning of this text and consists of cultivating the altruistic attitude of wishing to attain enlightenment for the sake of benefiting as many beings as possible, to the maximum extent. This is the bodhicitta motivation. As for the correct dedication, the function of this concluding practice is to ensure that whatever wealth of virtue has been accumulated by your dharma activities is not wasted or exhausted but rather is increased abundantly. Even if your collection of virtue is small, its fruit can be plentiful if the dedication is performed properly.

The results of meritorious actions depends a great deal upon your manner of dedicating them. If your previously accumulated wholesome actions are dedicated towards enlightenment, then they will definitely become the cause of attaining perfect buddhahood. If dedicated towards personal liberation from suffering, they will become the cause of your attaining nirvana. And if dedicated for the sake of this life's enjoyments, their results will follow accordingly. However, this last dedication is not a pure one and the one before that is not a sublime dedication. It is the first dedication that is the purest and most sublime of all. Therefore, whatever virtuous actions have been performed and whatever meritorious energy has been accumulated through them should be dedicated to the attainment of enlightenment for the sake of all sentient beings without exception.

Here, then, all the virtue of receiving and listening to mahamudra teachings, of reading mahamudra texts, of contemplating the meaning of mahamudra and of meditating upon the mahamudra stages of practice should be dedicated towards the achievement of that mahamudra which is the union of no more learning—the perfect enlightenment of buddhahood—for the sake of benefiting all others. Such a dedication is extremely important. If it is done correctly and sincerely from the depths of the heart, then the three-fold practice of hearing, thinking about and meditating upon these mahamudra teachings will be very meaningful and the source of great bliss.

Appendix 1: Prayer to the Gurus of the Mahamudra Lineage

Homage to the Great Seal

O pervasive master, the great Vajradhara
You who are the chief of all families and a buddha of the first glory,
Residing in the palace of the spontaneous three bodies,
To you I make these requests:
May I be able to cut the continuum of self-grasping,
May I be able to train in love, compassion and the mind of
   enlightenment,
May you transform me by your inspiring strength
To reach the unsurpassable mahamudra union swiftly through the
   paths.

O excellent, omniscient, superior Manjushri,
The father who gives birth to the conquerors of the three times
In the myriad fields throughout the ten directions of the world,
To you I make these requests:
May I be able to cut....

O reverend Losang Dragpa (Je Tsong-khapa),
You who are the second lord of Shakyamuni's doctrine
Here in the northern land of the snowy country,
To you I make these requests:
May I be able to cut....

Yong-dzin Trijang Dorje-chang

O Togden Jampel Gyatso
You who are the main holder of the doctrine of the attainment
  lineage
Of Je Tsong-khapa himself, the son of Manjushri,
To you I make these requests:
May I be able to cut....

O Baso Chökyi Gyaltsen,
You who have ripened all fortunate disciples
Having opened the treasure of the ear-whispered instructions,
To you I make these requests:
May I be able to cut....

O supreme yogi Dharma Vajra,
You who have found the knowledge-holding body of immortality
Having completed the yoga of the two tantric stages,
To you I make these requests:
May I be able to cut....

O Losang Dönyö Drubpa (Gyalwa Ensapa),
You who are untainted by the bondage of the eight worldly dharmas
And hold the banner of the definitive meaning's doctrine,
To you I make these requests:
May I be able to cut....

O Kedrub Sangye Yeshe,
You who guide all migrating beings by your dance of saffron
  robes
In the most joyous and splendid palace of three bodies,
To you I make these requests:
May I be able to cut....

O reverened Losang Chögyen (First Panchen Lama),
You who know all the doctrines of the lord conqueror Losang
  Dragpa,
Being no different from the protector,
To you I make these requests:
May I be able to cut....

O great yogi Gedun Gyaltsen (Nächu Rabjampa),
You who have completed the practices having integrated all the
  buddhas' words
Of sutra, tantra and shastra without exception into one meaning,

To you I make these requests:
May I be able to cut....

O yogi Gyaltsen Dzinpa (Drungpa Tsöndru Gyaltsen),
You who have found unique buddhahood by experiencing the
    essence
Of lord Je Tsong-khapa's doctrine with great enthusiasm,
To you I make these requests:
May I be able to cut....

O holder of the great lineage, Könchog Gyaltsen,
You who are so skilful in expounding the essence
Of the profound and vast nectar of the precious dharma
To those who are most fortunate disciples,
To you I make these requests:
May I be able to cut....

O reverend Losang Yeshe (Second Panchen Lama),
You who are lord Losang Chögyen himself,
Who have successfully revisited for the sake of the glorious doctrine
    and migrating beings,
To you I make these requests:
May I be able to cut....

O reverend Losang Trinley (Lhapa Tulku),
You who are so profoundly endowed with the ear-whispered lineage
And transformed by the inspiring strength of the actual buddhas,
To you I make these requests:
May I be able to cut....

O supreme yogi Drub-wang Losang Namgyal,
You who have completed the practice of the essential meaning
Of lord Je Tsong-khapa's ear-whispered instructions,
To you I make these requests:
May I be able to cut....

O kind Kachen Yeshe Gyaltsen,
You who have compassionately elucidated all the ear-whispered
    instructions
Of the lord gurus and their meaning without mistake,
To you I make these requests:
May I be able to cut....

O reverend Phurchog Ngawang Jampa,
You who have worked to spread the complete and flawless
Path of the quintessential doctrines throughout the central lands
  and border regions,
To you I make these requests:
May I be able to cut....

O great pandit Palden Yeshe (Third Panchen Lama),
You who have ripened all of China and Tibet through the dharma
With the saffron-robed buddha dance of first glory,
To you I make these requests:
May I be able to cut....

O Kedrub Ngawang Dorje,
You who have completed the attainments of all the noble paths
Of sutra and secret mantra by single-pointed concentration,
To you I make these requests:
May I be able to cut....

O reverend Ngul-chu Dharmabhadra,
You who are the protector of the dissemination of the buddhaharma
Through your expounding and composing and are like a second
  Shakyamuni,
Using means of skill and steadfastness,
To you I make these requests:
May I be able to cut....

O Yangchen Drubpay Dorje,
You whose profound and wide exquisite wisdom is like that of
Manjushri,
And who, out of great compassion beyond comprehension, never
  close your eyes,
To you I make these requests:
May I be able to cut....

O Kedrub Tenzin Tsöndru,
You who have gone to the city of union
And have completed the yoga of emptiness and bliss,
To you I make these requests:
May I be able to cut....

O Losang Drungpa Tsöndru Gyaltsen,

You who hold the banner of the doctrine of explanation and
  attainment
And have completed the realization of the profound paths,
To you I make these requests:
May I be able to cut. . . .

O Losang Dönyö Drubpa,
You who hold the essence of the doctrine of the three trainings
And are untainted by the defilements of faults and downfalls,
To you I make these requests:
May I be able to cut. . . .

O reverend Drub-Kangpa Geleg Gyatso,
You who are the second conqueror, the lord Losang Dragpa,
Who again manifested the dance of the saffron-robed monk,
To you I make these requests:
May I be able to cut. . . .

O kind Phurchog Ngawang Jampa,
You who have illuminated the treasure of the doctrine
Of the profound and extensive path to all fortunate ones,
To you I make these requests:
May I be able to cut. . . .

O sublime and wise Jamyang Shaypa Könchog Jigmey Wangpo,
You who are proficient in illuminating the noble paths
Free from extremes through your loud laughter of stainless logic,
To you I make these requests:
May I be able to cut. . . .

O reverend (Gung-tang) Tenpey Drönmey,
You who are peerless in your propagation of the explanations and
  attainments
Constituting the paramount system of the victorious noble-minded
  one,
To you I make these requests:
May I be able to cut. . . .

O reverend Könchog Gyaltsen (Amdo Pelmang),
You whose strong body of experiential realization is greatly
  developed
Through tasting the protector lord Manjushri's nectar-like ear-
  whispered lineage,

To you I make these requests:
May I be able to cut....

O great yogi Ngödrub Rabten,
You who hold single-pointedly the banner of the doctrine
Of the attainment lineage in not one fixed place only,
To you I make these requests:
May I be able to cut....

O tutor (Tha-tsay) Gedun Gyatso,
You who have completed the excellences of abandonment and
    realization
And caused to descend the dharma-rain of good explanations for
    living beings,
To you I make these requests:
May I be able to cut....

O glorious Tenpey Nyima,
You who have reached every high attainment of the two tantric
    stages
And were crowned among all the wise of supreme omniscience,
To you I make these requests:
May I be able to cut....

O most reverend Trinley Gyatso (Phabongkha Rinpoche),
You who upheld the banner of both sutra and secret mantra
By the power of your loving kindness towards all migrating beings,
To you I make these requests:
May I be able to cut....

O most kind Losang Yeshe (Trijang Rinpoche),
You who are the spiritual master enhancing fortunate disciples
And the essence of the second lord conqueror's heart,
To you I make these requests:
May I be able to cut....

O most developed Thubten Lungtog (Ling Rinpoche),
You who increase all the doctrines of Shakyamuni's scriptures
    and realizations
As was the conqueror's intention,
To you I make these requests:
May I be able to cut....

O my most kind root gurus,
You who gloriously appear for the sake of faithful disciples
At the seat of the former venerable yogis,
To you I make these requests:
May I be able to cut the continuum of self-grasping,
May I be able to train in love, compassion and the mind of
   enlightenment,
May you transform me by your inspiring strength
To reach the unsurpassable mahamudra union swiftly through the
   paths.

May I be able to behold my venerable gurus as buddhas,
May I be able to develop disgust for this samsaric environment,
Having taken the burden of releasing all my mother migrating beings
Through the paths of the mundane and supramundane,
May you transform me by your inspiring strength
To reach speedily that exquisite union of mahamudra.

This body of mine and your body, O Father,
This speech of mine and your speech, O Father,
This mind of mine and your heart, O Father—
By your inspiring strength transform my three doors
To become inseparably the same as yours.

Yong-dzin Ling Dorje-chang

Appendix 2: Outline of the Text

Notes

Foreword

1 Yong-dzin Ling Rinpoche pays homage here to Je Tsong-khapa
and refers to him by his ordination name Losang Dragpa (Skt.
Sumati Kirti). The three sets of vows are the pratimoksha vows of
individual liberation, the bodhisattva vows and the secret mantra
vows.

2 'Joyous' is the translation of Ganden (Skt. Tushita), the name
of the monastery near Lhasa founded by Je Tsong-khapa. Thus the
phrase 'the Joyous mahamudra' refers to those mahamudra teachings
passed down in a lineage traceable through Je Tsong-khapa back to
Buddha Vajradhara.

Introduction

3 In this text 'yogi' is used in reference to both male and female
practitioners of secret mantra despite the fact that the proper
feminine form of this Sanskrit term is 'yogini'.

4 Such technical terms as 'white drop' and 'simultaneous great
bliss' will be explained later in this text.

5 In this context 'mandala' refers to a circular diagram of the
universe which is symbolically offered to the gurus, or spiritual
masters, of the mahamudra lineage. Such an offering is generally
accompanied by the recitation of a prayer such as the following:

By directing to the fields of buddhas
This offering of a mandala built on a base

Resplendent with flowers, saffron water and incense,
Adorned with Mount Meru and the four continents
As well as the sun and the moon,
May all sentient beings be led to these fields.

6   Some of the works in which these preliminary practices have
been explained are listed in the bibliography. Of special interest in
this regard are Geshe Rabten's *The Preliminary Practices* and Brian
Beresford's translation entitled *Mahayana Purification.*

Chapter Two
7   The names Vajravarahi (Diamond Sow) and Vajrayogini
(Diamond Practitioner) refer to the same female deity, the former
term emphasizing her function and the latter her essence. In reality,
Vajrayogini is the wisdom of the inseparability of simultaneous great
bliss and emptiness. Because such wisdom functions to destroy the
confusion—symbolized by a pig—resulting from the ignorant
conception of inherent existence, this deity is also known as Vajravarahi.
8   Vairochana is the buddha of the purified aggregate of form.
The seven parts of the posture associated with this buddha concern
the position of the legs, back, shoulders, arms and hands, head, eyes
and mouth. Anyone seriously interested in secret mantra meditation
should receive a practical demonstration of this posture from a
qualified teacher.
9   Some texts, when explaining the inner fire meditation according to the practice of Vajrayogini, identify the letter in the throat
channel-wheel as *aṁ*.
10   The three times are the past, present and future and the ten
directions are the four cardinal and four intermediate directions, the
zenith and nadir. Thus the phrase 'three times and ten directions'
means 'all times and everywhere'.

Chapter Three
11   The wording of the following explanation has been adapted
from the discussion found in Lati Rinbochay and Hopkins, pp.
38-41.
12   For a more complete discussion of death, the intermediate
state and rebirth consult Lati Rinbochay and Hopkins.

Chapter Five

13   For a complete listing of the six primary consciousnesses and the fifty-one mental factors consult Geshe Rabten's *The Mind and Its Functions* and Guenther and Kawamura's *Mind in Buddhist Psychology.*

14   According to some texts there is another way of classifying the three levels of mind. In them the five sense consciousnesses are said to be the gross level of mind, the eighty indicative conceptions are the subtle level and the four empties (from the white appearance to the clear light) are the very subtle level of mind.

Chapter Six

15   For more detailed instructions on tranquil abiding meditation consult Wallace's *The Life and Teaching of Geshe Rabten*, pp. 165-187 and Geshe Kelsang Gyatso's *Meaningful to Behold* (a commentary to Shantideva's *Guide to the Bodhisattva's Way of Life*), pp. 223-234.

Chapter Seven

16   For detailed analyses of Chandrakirti and Shantideva's classic statements of the Madhyamika-Prasangika view of emptiness see Wilson's *Chandrakirti's Sevenfold Reasoning* and Geshe Kelsang Gyatso's *Meaningful to Behold*. See also the Dalai Lama's *The Buddhism of Tibet and the Key to the Middle Way* and Hopkins' *Meditation on Emptiness.*

Chapter Eight

17   Praises by the Eighth Karmapa and others testifying to Je Tsong-khapa's mastery of sutra and secret mantra can be found in Mullin's *Four Songs to Je Rinpoche.*

Glossary and Index

The page references given here are not intended to be exhaustive but rather indicate the first or the major appearances of each term.

Tibetan Names of Texts

Clear Lamp of the Five stages (Chandrakirti): Rim pa lnga'i sgron gsal.

Commentary to the Treasury of Instruction (Long-chen-pa): Man ngag mdzod 'grel.

Excellent Path of Liberation (Keu-tsang): rNam grol lam bzang.

Five Stages of the Completion Stage (Nagarjuna): rDzogs rim gyi rim pa lnga.

Four Hundred (Aryadeva): bZhi brgya pa.

Great Drum Sutra: rNga bo che'i mdo.

Great Exposition of the Stages of the Path (Tsong-khapa): Lam rim chen mo.

Great Exposition of the Stages of the Path of Secret Mantra (Tsong-khapa): aNgags rim chen mo.

Guhyasamaja Root Tantra: gSang ba 'dus pa'i rtsa rgyud.

Guide to the Bodhisattva's Way of Life (Shantideva): Byang chub sems pa'i spyod pa la 'jug pa.

Guide to the Middle Way (Chandrakirti): dBu ma la 'jug pa.

Heruka Root Tantra: He ru ka rtsa rgyud.

Hevajra Root Tantra: Kye rdorgyi rtsa rgyud.

Jewel Ornament of Liberation (Gam-po-pa): Nor bu thar pa rin po che'i rgyan.

King of Concentrations Sutra: Ting nge 'dzin rgyal po'i mdo.

Lamp of Condensed Deeds (Aryadeva): sPyod pa 'dus pa'i sgron ma.

Lamp of Re-illumination (Panchen Losang Chögyen): Yang gsal sgron me.

Lamp of the Clear Excellent Path of the Ear-whispered Lineage (Kachen Yeshe Gyaltsen): sNyan rgyud lam bzang gsal ba'i sgron me.

Lamp of the Path to Enlightenment (Atisha): Byang chub lam gyi sgron ma.

Lamp Thoroughly Illuminating the Five Stages (Tsong-khapa): Rim pa lnga rab tu gsal ba'i sgron me.

Little Samvara Tantra: rGyud sdom chung.

Main Path of the Conquerors (Panchen Losang Chögyen): rGyal ba'i gzhung lam.

Ocean of Actual Attainment (Kedrub Je): dNgos grub rgya mtsho.

Offering to the Spiritual Master (Panchen Losang Chögyen): Bla ma mchod pa.

Ornament of Clear Realizations (Maitreya): mNgon par rtogs pa'i rgyan.

Perfection of Wisdom Sutra: Sher phyin gyi mdo.

Samputa Tantra: Yang tag par spyor ba zhes bya ba'i rgyud.

Six Practices (Naropa): Na ro chos drug.

Stages of Instruction from the Approach of the Profound Path of Naropa's Six Practices Called the Three Convictions (Tsong-khapa): Zab lam na ro'i chos drug gi sgo nas 'khrid pa'i rim pa yid ches gsum ldan zhes bya ba.

Wisdom Vajra Compendium (Aryadeva): Ye shes rdo rje kun las btus pa.

Vinaya Pitaka: 'Dul ba'i sde snod.

Bibliography

Beresford, B. (trans.). *Mahayana Purification*. Dharamsala: LTWA, 1980.

Berzin, A. (trans.). *The Mahamudra Eliminating the Darkness of Ignorance* by the Ninth Karmapa. Dharamsala: LTWA, 1978.

Conze, E. (trans.). *The Perfection of Wisdom in Eight Thousand Lines*. Bolinas: Four Seasons Foundation, 1973.

Tenzin Gyatso, the Fourteenth Dalai Lama. *The Buddhism of Tibet and the Key to the Middle Way*. London: George Allen & Unwin, 1975.

Evans-Wentz, W.Y. (ed.). *Tibetan Yoga and Secret Doctrines*. London: Oxford University Press, 1935.

Gampopa. *The Jewel Ornament of Liberation* (trans. Guenther). London: Rider, 1959.

Guenther, H.V. (trans.). *The Life and Teaching of Naropa*. London: OUP, 1963.

_____ *The Royal Song of Saraha*. Berkeley: Shambhala, 1973.

Guenther, H.V. and Kawamura, L.S. (trans.). *Mind in Buddhist Psychology*. Emeryville: Dharma, 1975.

Geshe Kelsang Gyatso. *Meaningful to Behold*. Ulverston: Wisdom Publications, 1980.

Hopkins, J. *Meditation on Emptiness*. Forthcoming.

_____ (trans.). *Tantra in Tibet*. London: George Allen & Unwin, 1977.

Lati Rinbochay and Hopkins, J. (trans.). *Death, Intermediate State and Rebirth in Tibetan Buddhism*. London: Rider, 1979.

Mullin, G. (trans.). *Four Songs to Je Rinpoche*. Dharamsala: LTWA, 1978.

Geshe Rabten. *The Mind and Its Functions*. Mt. Pelerin: Tharpa Choeling, 1978.

———— *The Preliminary Practices*. Dharamsala: LTWA, 1974.

Wallace, B.A. (trans.). *The Life and Teaching of Geshe Rabten*. London: George Allen & Unwin, 1980.

Wilson, J. *Chandrakirti's Sevenfold Reasoning: Meditation on the Selflessness of Persons*. Dharamsala: LTWA, 1980